Let the Spirit Shape Your Ministries

*40 Reflections of a Veteran Pastor
and Organizational Psychologist*

DAVID S. LUECKE

WESTBOW
PRESS®
A DIVISION OF THOMAS NELSON
& ZONDERVAN

WestBow Press books may be ordered through booksellers or by contacting:

WestBow Press
A Division of Thomas Nelson & Zondervan
1663 Liberty Drive
Bloomington, IN 47403
www.westbowpress.com
844-714-3454

Scripture taken from the Holy Bible, New International Version®.
NIV®. Copyright © 1973, 1978, 1984 by International Bible Society.
Used by permission of Zondervan. All rights reserved.

ISBN: 978-1-6642-9412-7 (sc)
ISBN: 978-1-6642-9413-4 (e)

Library of Congress Control Number: 2023904109

Print information available on the last page.

WestBow Press rev. date: 05/31/2023

Contents

Overview of Ministry Challenges Today

Part I   Name, Share and Seek More of the Spirit
Naming the Spirit at Work in Lives

Sharing Spirit Experiences with Others

Seek Growth in the Spirit's Influence

Part II   The Spirit Calls, Gathers, Enlightens, and Sanctifies

The Spirit Calls

The Spirit Gathers

The Spirit Enlightens

The Spirit Sanctifies

Conclusions

Where Did the Spirit Go?

Something major is happening among Christian churches in American, specifically the traditional mainline denominations of Episcopalian, Lutheran, Presbyterian, Reformed and Methodist. We have been declining for 50 years, and the decline is accelerating. Why? More importantly, what can we do about turning decline around?

Based on doing pastoral ministry for thirty-five years, I know the problems and challenges first-hand. After seminary, I was a business school professor and then spent years trying to help congregations learn to better manage their ministries through my writings, workshops and ten years of teaching a Doctor of Ministry course on church management. I no longer think better management is the solution. A decade ago, I re-oriented my thinking toward greater appreciation of the Holy Spirit and his impact on church life. He is the missing element in so much writing and consulting on better church leadership.

The forty Reflections presented here had their origins in the 120 blogs I wrote and sent out to over 6,000 on my contact list and to various Facebook and LinkedIn groups. My website is WhatHappened. church. These Reflections are my attempt to integrate my thinking and make basic insights accessible to those in traditional, mainline churches and to do so without theological and church jargon.

Part 1 of these Reflections will address how to recognize the Spirit at work, then the importance of sharing Spirit sightings, and finally personal practices you can do to be drawn closer to God. You can't really get a congregation better involved in the Spirit's work until you appreciate how the Spirit has worked in your own life.

Part 2 will be based on Martin Luther's explanation of the Spirit's role in the Trinity. He calls, gathers, enlightens and sanctifies God's people. Those are basic functions of routine ministry in a congregation. We tend to think ministry is something we do. But we are really on a team, and the team leader is Christ's Spirit.

Jesus taught that the Spirit is unpredictable; he is like that wind that blows where it will. We know he always works through God's Word. But the fact is that the ways biblical insights are best shared does change over time. Tens of thousands of congregations are still doing ministries the same way they did fifty years ago. Where did the people go? Where did the Spirit go?

Church decline would be easier to understand if it was happening to all Protestant congregations. But we are witnessing fresh growth in the non-denominational community churches that are thriving in so many areas. What can we learn?

The Head Rules the Belly Through the Chest

Consider an insight from C.S. Lewis, as interpreted by seminary professor Jeff Dryden. He highlights Lewis' metaphor that "the head rules the belly through the chest." The chest is the heart seen as the seat of emotions. The belly is irrational passions. The chest has to be trained to love what the head recognizes as good, otherwise it will not have the power to overcome the passions.

Dryden confesses that he is of generation of theology students who were trained in head truths. He is a Presbyterian. That's my experience as a Lutheran. There was a time when I could recite the history of doctrinal developments over twenty centuries of Christian theology. But then came the realization, Who cares? The traditional assumption was that right knowledge will lead to right behavior. From a psychological viewpoint this approach seems astonishingly naïve. This rationalistic formation model doesn't work for humans because we are not thinking-willing machines. It produces "men without chests" of passions.

As a corrective Dryden finds himself drawn to the spiritual formation movement. But too often that leads to men without heads because of its focus on emotions. The challenge in theological education is to get head and chest in the right relationship. That is best done with examples of teachers who personify the right balance. He offers the simple but powerful observation that "We cannot take students somewhere we have not been."

My big take-away from years of pastoral ministry is that the basic job is to help participants grow closer to God, to become more like Christ. In my heritage that is called sanctification, being made holy. We are squeamish about focusing on sanctification lest it be confused with justification, being made righteous before God. That's why we end up taking a rational approach to teaching discipleship. This is what the disciples did; therefore, this is what you should do. How well does that work? "Should" is never a good motivator.

It's not possible to promote better discipleship without a good understanding of the Holy Spirit. The Spirit provides the missing link between being made just and becoming more like Christ. The Spirit changes our inner being and energizes new motivations. The new life is the Spirit-infused life that wants to serve and witness to others.

Use "energy" as a good word to describe the health of a church. Thank God for congregations that have developed energized ministries. But worry about those what seem to have run out of energy in general. They have inevitably run out of basic spiritual energy. It is easy for congregations to slide into become just another social organization, but with a veneer of holy words. Most such social clubs are now fast declining, too.

So how do you get a Christian church "re-energized"? The process starts with the leader. Like theology professors cannot take students somewhere they themselves have never been, so pastors cannot take a congregation where they personally have never been.

There is hope for aging, declining congregations. But don't look for a simple formula or easy program. Re-energizing is the slow process of enriching personal spiritual lives. Even when there is no growth in number of participants, there can be soul-satisfying growth in the Spirit's fruit of love, joy, peace and hope.

Show me a passionate congregation, and you will find a passionate pastor. You will also see plenty of evidence of the Spirit at work.

Re-Discovering the Holy Spirit

Every congregation has some. These are mature Christians well along in their journey of becoming more like Christ. When asked, others can usually point them out by name. What they convey is fruit the Holy Spirit has produced in them. The Apostle Paul lists some, like love, joy, peace, patience. Under the influence of the Spirit, these inner qualities often flourish in individual spiritual journeys over the years. How does that happen?

Most communities now have some. These are new community churches which seem to be growing and even flourishing. Most are conservative and solidly Gospel-oriented in their ministries. For those believers primed to see the Holy Spirit at work, many of these congregations give evidence of the Spirit moving with special energy. They are "happening" places.

Meanwhile, the traditional mainline churches (Episcopalian, Lutheran, Presbyterian, Reformed, Methodist) seem to be sitting on the side-lines grumpily watching their continued fifty-year decline in membership and influence. So long as they stay anchored in God's Word, they retain the Spirit in their midst. But too often the Spirit gets harder to recognize. Many were exciting and dynamic congregations that did valuable Christian ministry in their day. But too often the "happening" Spirit seems to have moved on.

Pastoring a declining church can be very discouraging. Surveys show that a large and increasing share of pastors are facing burnout. The percentage of those who leave the ministry is increasing. Where is the joy of ministry? When you are trying to do ministry with just your own energy and see fewer results you think are important, satisfying joy becomes harder to find.

But recognize that church ministry is basically the Holy Spirit's work. You are part of his team, and he is the team leader. The Spirit wants to open your personal eyes to his presence and movement around you in ways more subtle than can easily be counted. In the process, you may discover more personal joy in what your team is accomplishing.

Martin Luther taught that the Spirit's special role in the Trinity is to "call, gather, enlighten and sanctify" the whole church. To call includes presenting the Gospel in new ways that meet the changed felt needs of others in our times. To gather involves bringing people into Christ-focused fellowships that go beyond church membership. To be enlightened happens as much with what is caught as with what is taught. To sanctify involves personal journeys of becoming more like Christ. Find joy in those journeys of others. Find satisfaction and joy in your own personal journey.

How the Spirit Got Lost

For centuries the Holy Spirit was relegated to the side-lines in traditional Protestant churches. We confessed him in the Creeds but took little notice of him in our daily lives and church ministries. We did not have need for his special contribution. The Spirit came roaring back into Protestant consciousness in the emotional Pentecostal movement starting a century ago that is now spreading mightily around the world in our times. Rejoice that the Word of the Lord is growing faster now than at any time in the previous two-thousand year of the Christian church's existence.

Yet the older church bodies anchored on their Reformation heritage hesitate to join the celebration. The theology we inherited is very head oriented, and we are reluctant to address feelings or emotions that might lead astray. Yet churches without passion become apathetic and decline.

We can better appreciate emotions by recognizing that Feelings can and should come at the end of the sequence of three Fs. Start with relying on biblical Facts. Then comes trusting them in Faith. In third place is the response of Feelings. Facts without Feelings can be as dead as Faith without Works. How can a believer not be moved emotionally when the Facts of the Gospel are well understood and trusted?

The churches now in decline used to be called the mainline denominations. Our roots are in Northern Europe. People of those lands typically are not as comfortable expressing emotions as those from other cultures. We traditional churches of the Reformation need to recognize we are on the defensive in this world. What we can do is learn how to help members readily express their feelings and passions in response to the Gospel they trust.

The challenge I am addressing is how we get back on the offensive with a fuller understanding of how the Holy Spirit is at work in our midst today. Call it a working theology. The place to start is Jesus' own teaching. He explained to Nicodemus that the Holy Spirit influences human spirit. The Spirit actually changes our inner being (John 3). *Where* the Spirit brings special energy at any given time is unpredictable, like the wind. *How* he influences people always remains the same. He works through God's Word and the means by which this word of grace is conveyed, like the Sacraments. We can look for the Spirit at work in Word-centered relationships that are basic to ministry.

Jesus taught his disciples that the Father will send another Advocate, whom they will know "because he lives with you and will be in you." This Advocate, the Holy Spirit, "will remind you of everything I have said to you" (John 14). We do not look for the Spirit as somehow independent from the Father and Son in the Trinity. Jesus explained, He will not speak on his own authority (John 16).

A thousand years ago, the Christian church split over the issue of whether the Holy Spirit proceeds from the Father or from both the Father and the Son. Far from being an obscure theological debate, the question is very relevant to our understanding how the Spirit works in our lives today. The Greek term for the Holy Spirit is Paraclete, one who comes alongside. A very good translation is Advocate, like a lawyer who advocates the case of his client. The Spirit advocates for the will of the Father and the Son in our personal lives.

Thus, the Holy Spirit is not a free-floating spirit off on his own somewhere intervening in people's lives about whatever interests them.

The Holy Spirit is confined to advocating the will of the Father and the Son. He manifests himself in people's lives through working out the love of the Father and applying the grace offered in Jesus Christ. He will not advocate what is contrary to God's Word.

The Holy Spirit is Christ's Spirit, as Paul explicitly identifies him. Christ's Spirit and the Holy Spirit are interchangeable. They are like a two-sided coin. Jesus Christ did his redemptive work 2,000 years ago. Ascended, he is now present with us working through his Spirit.

Re-Tooling for the Post-Modern Culture

The prophet Ezekiel gave us the image of the Word of the Lord breathing new life into old, dry bones. He assured, "I will put my Spirit in you and you will live" (Ezekiel 37). Traditional churches are in danger of seeing their bones go dry in our times. We need the Spirit to refresh us. The way he does is as old as Scriptures. The Spirit works through God's inspired Word and the relationships based on it. As Ezekiel said, "Dry bones, hear the word of the Lord. The Sovereign Lord says, I will put breath into you, and you will come to life."

Churches open to new ways of expressing the Spirit's movement face new opportunities in our changing American culture

Three American Cultures in 80 Years

In the old American culture, Christian churches fit comfortably. There was no pressing *need* for the Holy Spirit. The 1960s brought the dominance of the Modern Scientific Culture, in which there was no *room* for the Spirit. The present Post-Modern Culture is wide *open* to the spirit world and the Holy Spirit's work. Opportunities abound for churches that follow the Spirit's lead.

The Sacred Canopy existed as the dominant American culture for the centuries through World War II. Religious and social life fit together. Sociologist Peter Berger gave us the phrase "Sacred Canopy" to describe a society of shared fundamental assumptions. Over 80% of Americans would check that they are Christians. Life was created by God, and we defined ourselves by our relationship to this God who sets our morality of responsibilities to him and to each other. Life revolved around sin and salvation. Churches were a dominant and valued part of social life.

The Modern, Scientific Culture appeared at the popular level in the 1960s when rational assumptions were increasingly applied to all of life. In this world view there is no place for the supernatural. You could have your own beliefs, but they are not relevant to what counts. Those who take the Bible seriously were viewed as fundamentalists who really don't belong in the progressive world.

In this modern culture, ministers in mainline denominations learned the new academic rules for interpreting the Bible. There is no significant supernatural world. Miracles need to be explained away. The Bible is a collection of literature that has no special divinely inspired authority. Churches were regarded as social organizations that need to justify themselves by the social purposes they pursue. Progressive churches oriented themselves to the modern secular world. But many forfeited much of the spiritual world. Churches that went liberal are the ones in steepest decline now.

The Post-Modern Culture is the one in which most young people now live. By training and occupation, they are immersed in the scientific culture. But they are looking for something more. What can be empirically proven is not providing a fulfilling life for them. They are open to worlds beyond observable nature, that is, the supernatural. What they are groping for could be called spiritual meaning. But they don't carry the assumptions of the old Sacred Canopy culture. Most don't see the Bible as having any special authority. They are resistant to institutional churches that define themselves by their beliefs and traditions. They are looking for religious groups that define themselves by their actions and the quality of their community life.

What are the touchpoints for reaching out to Post-Moderns? This is the driving question for traditional churches looking for a better future. The challenge is to address their felt lack of meaning and their loneliness. Because they are open to the supernatural, they can be interested in how the Holy Spirit changes lives. They are looking for evidence of the Spirit, not a theology of the Spirit. They are not looking initially for ethical rules and guilt based on them. A loving God of grace who accepts them as they are makes sense. They are open to informal church communities that reflect life and relationships open to the Spirit.

The Growing Community Churches

Many traditional churches are neighbors to newer growing community churches that choose to identify themselves as non-denominational. What an odd way and clever way to stand out, by comparing themselves to the older denominational churches that are beginning to look worn out. The older church bodies defined themselves primarily by their beliefs, as those were carefully formulated in previous centuries. Besides announcing their newness, community churches are branding themselves by the actions of their ministries focused on their community.

These newer churches do associate themselves with different movements or networks of like-minded churches. By their very nature, community churches do not have a reporting mechanism that totals combined attendance. Judging by the growth I witness, my guess is that their growing attendance just about makes up for the decline in traditional denominational churches in recent years.

My hunch is that many participants in the new community churches are spiritually healthier because their involvement is a personal choice. The older denominational churches have many for whom participation is an expression of a church culture shaped over generations. Faith rooted in a shared culture can be exciting and uplifting. But it can also be shallow, epitomized by Christmas & Easter Christians. As the underlying social culture disintegrates, those with only culture-shaped faith find their habits less compelling, and church life loses its appeal. Many of those traditional mainline churches adopted the approach of social clubs and organizations, which were also growing among new suburbanites looking for new friends and social relationships. Those organization, too, are now in steep decline.

There is much need for research on the growing community church movement. Meanwhile, I offer my own observations. With a few exceptions, most non-denominational churches present conservative biblically based beliefs that shape biblical living. They are strenuously outreach oriented. They strive for spontaneity and resist an institutional feel. The music is contemporary and upbeat. They support friendships and social interaction. They talk a lot about the Spirit and what God is doing. They are well organized, with supportive, low-visibility structures. Their leaders usually reflect an unrelenting focus and drive to help people grow as disciples of Christ.

Community churches strive to present themselves as "happening" places that bring spiritual value to those who participate. Traditional mainline churches too often seem like they are meant for somebody else, and their best days are behind them.

Re-Tooling Traditional Church Life

The most basic step for bringing fresh breath to old churches is to raise mission outreach in their congregational priorities. Then look at how other energetic churches have developed their ministries. Adapt what you can. Often this means starting new worship styles.

Reaching Post-Moderns means showing an intense interest in each personally and demonstrating what a Spirit-driven community can offer. Such ministry is very time-consuming. It can best be done by young adults who develop a passion, show aptitude, and learn by doing. The best older members can do is to clear the way, raise up and then support the new generation of leaders.

Fresh Behavioral Perspectives on Ministry

Consider fresh perspectives on the challenge of re-tooling our inherited ministries. And the emphasis today indeed needs to be on ministries, not just academic theology alone. Theologians like to make distinctions, but if a distinction doesn't make a difference in ministry, why pursue it?

Social anthropologists define a culture as a set of beliefs, values and behaviors passed on to a new generation. The reality now is that new generations in our times are not concerned so much about beliefs as they are about behaviors and the values they reflect. This observation about shifting values holds especially true for today's traditional church cultures, where young generations have mostly gone missing.

Organizational Psychology focuses on motivation—what moves people into action. This approach starts with the simple assumption that people act to fill needs important to them at a given time. Immigrant churches could count on loyalty from participants who have a high need for security in a new land. Then, many suburbanites were attracted to new church plants out of a need for social affiliation, and they fashioned their church cultures after other social organizations. Younger generations have newer ways to satisfy their social needs.

Organizational Behavior recognizes that informal fellowships of believers don't last long without adding some sort of formal structure to handle problems that arise and cause conflict. The issue is whether the people serve the organization, or does the formal structure serve the people. Poorly organized congregations can turn into crusty institutions that too often strangle the life out of the underlying fellowship of Christ followers. When believers say they want no part of organized religion, they are saying they had bad experiences with overbearing leaders working through inadequate structures.

Marketing is another fresh perspective I bring, having taught it and strategic management for years as Professor of Administrative Sciences. Corporate strategies depend on defining and expanding their market of those who will consume their product. Businesses die when they lose their market. So do churches.

Traditional churches of the Reformation inherited a church culture where their people were captive in their village setting. The job of pastors was to educate them in what to believe and do. In the process preachers too often relied on applying heavy doses of guilt, shaming them into proper God-pleasing behavior.

The fresh community churches do not carry that kind of cultural left-over with them. They typically plant new churches that assume little loyalty. Their challenge is to recognize needs of those they are reaching out to and then to offer ministries that fill those needs. This is straight marketing language. But in corporations the marketers need to be balanced by engineers who assure the product will work. So, too, glib marketers of spiritual themes need biblical engineering to clarify that the Spirit they proclaim is the one sent by the righteous God who offers redemption in Jesus Christ. Where even just a portion God's Word is proclaimed, we can hope that the Spirit creates in those participants a hunger for greater substance and for a church fellowship where that is offered.

The "market" for finding more meaning and purpose in life remains strong in our society and is indeed growing, especially among the Post-Modern generations. The ministry challenge is to fine-tune mainline church ministries to feature Christ in language and behaviors young adults can more readily identify with.

Hope for Dying Congregations

Is there hope for dying congregations that are on the defensive today? Yes. Pay more attention to the Spirit's energizing work in your midst. Pray for his presence. The Spirit works basically through relationships. Emphasize grace-focused, Spirit-shaped fellowship among those already gathered. Have a heart for reaching out to others in creative ways. Pray for momentum in your ministries. Then work hard to keep up with where the Spirit is moving. That's the leadership challenge.

Jesus explained to Nicodemus that the Spirit influences human spirit. He compared this Spirit to the wind, which blows wherever it pleases. To his disciples, Jesus named the dilemma his followers face. "The world cannot accept the Spirit because it neither sees him nor knows him." Paul explained that the eyes of the heart have to be enlightened to see the Spirit's work. What a quandary! The argument is circular that it takes the Spirit to recognize the Spirit. But that's the spiritual reality we face.

Many in traditional churches don't know the Spirit well. We can carefully lay out our ministry ambitions and determine what we want God's Spirit to do. In our plans we like to give him assignments. Too often we are disappointed in the results. We want him to follow us. But the reality is we have to follow him.

Thirty-five years ago I co-authored the book *Pastoral Administration: Integrating Ministry and Management.* It sold well, especially among mainline churches. But it did little to turn around their decline. That book was at a time before I homed in on the Spirit's role in church life. Helpful for that was working through Gordon Fee's detailed analysis of the 169 references to the Spirit in Paul's letters. Its title is *God's Empowering Presence.* That was the dimension missing from a conventional management approach.

We can lay out our hopes and plans, but we cannot count on the Spirit to fit himself into of our intentions. What worked in past ministry will not necessarily work now. The Spirit may have moved on to work through other ministries better attuned to changing times. Better management alone will not halt the decline of traditional churches. Nor will pep talks. The answer is to become better hosts for the Spirit's work.

Where are the detailed construction documents for effective ministry? They remain sketchy so long as the unpredictable Spirit is involved. Think of building a porch as entryway into a house. We can draw out in detail what that porch should look like, complete with solid railings and sturdy steps. But constructing entranceways is not the ultimate objective for ministry in God's church. Our goal is to usher people into the house of experiencing a living relationship with God. It is Christ's Spirit who breathes life and brings growth into our encounters with God. The challenge is to build more functional porches that more effectively usher people into God's living presence.

Leaders with a heart for ministry are fundamental to healthy church life. A recent major research project with data from 1,000 Protestant congregations offered conclusions about what healthy congregations look like. Basic is that leadership matters. A key attribute for church leaders is an unrelenting, uncompromising focus and drive to help grow people into disciples of Christ. It's their hearts—consumed by Christ—that make the difference.

Effective ministry today is more than a church job. It has to be a passion. Sustained passion can only come from the Spirit.

Recognize When and How the Spirit Is At Work

From her study of two Vineyard Fellowships, Anthropologist T. M. Luhrmann concluded, "Coming to a committed belief in God was more like learning to do something than to think about something. I would describe what I saw as a theory of attentional learning—the way you pay attention determines your experience of God.

Clinical Psychologist J. Harold Ellens often witnessed the joy and satisfaction they expressed when his clients recognized God was influencing and changing them supernaturally. He concluded, "It is important to name those movements and tell others about them, so we become people of the Spirit, cultivating a culture of the Spirit."

Diane Butler Bass did presentations and discussions with mainline pastors. She observed that to put the words "experiential" and "belief" in the same sentence is asking for trouble in those circles. Noting how the modern Pentecostal movement first gave expression to the priority of experience, she reports the reaction of one pastor: "You mean we're all going to become Pentecostals? My congregation would rather die first! Faith isn't about feelings. It has to have intellectual content." Another said, "Why is it that the choice among churches always seems to be the choice between intelligence on ice and ignorance on fire?"

Moving the Middle

There is a middle ground between icy intellectual and fiery ignorance. The psalms point the way. Consider Psalm 23 "The Lord Is My Shepherd." What makes it so popular is its description of many feeling experiences. In the Lord I feel full and find peace. My anxious soul is refreshed. He gives me confidence. He takes away fear. My cup overflows with blessings. I trust him and feel his presence. Second most popular is Psalm 51 with its description of a crushed inner soul. Wash away my iniquity and cleanse me from my sin. Create in me a pure heart, God, and renew a steadfast spirit within me. Restore to me the joy of your salvation.

Traditional mainline worship is full of rational explanations of the faith, especially in heavily head-oriented sermons. Yet provision was made for heart-oriented feelings by the extensive us of psalms and hymns like "I Know that My Redeemer Lives" and "Beautiful Savior". Traditional worship did have a middle ground appropriate to its times. What's happening today is movement of that middle more to emotions of the heart. Some Pentecostal worship is almost raw emotions. Plenty traditional churches, though, are exploring worship with more subtle feelings.

For churches oriented to the Word, feelings need to be in a proper sequence of Facts, Faith and Feelings. *Facts* about God are proclaimed in the Word. *Faith* is not only the noun for beliefs but especially the verb for trusting those facts about God. God-pleasing *Feelings* then flow from such trust. Spiritual leaders can be more confident in their ministry when they expect the Holy Spirit to work through this progression of Facts, Faith and then Feelings.

Paul's Experiences of the Holy Spirit

The apostle Paul had a dramatic experience of God on the road to Damascus. Often overlooked is his slow over-the-years formation by the Spirit. According to Paul's report to the Galatians, a total of fourteen years passed after his conversion and before he joined with Barnabas on his first mission journey. Undoubtedly Paul spent a lot of his unrecorded years explaining to others what happened to him. In those years he worked out the centrality of grace in God's relationship with his people. He also came to much greater depth of understanding how the Spirit works changes in the believer's heart, as Spirit did in his own life.

When Paul wrote about what the Spirit can do among God's

people, you can confidently assume this is what the Spirit did to him. He learned to look into the future based on his own past experiences of the Spirit. You, too, can do that.

Have you found that your understanding of faith has moved beyond the basics to greater willingness to live with Jesus as Lord of your life? That was the Spirit at work. (1 Corinthians 12:3)

Have you experienced a lessening of fears that inhibit joyful living? The Spirit helps you become confident of yourself as God's child (Romans 8: 15).

Have you noticed yourself more inclined to be involved in your congregation, perhaps teaching Sunday School or taking on administrative responsibilities? The Holy Spirt has been working on you, giving you extra motivation to do what you now find satisfying (1Corinthians 12:7).

Have you found lately a greater sense of love, joy, peace and patience? That was the Sprit producing these fruit in your life (Galatians 5: 22).

Can you prove that any of these positive movements in your life came from the Holy Spirit? No more that you can prove God exists to someone who does not want to see him. These insights happen when the eyes of your heart are enlightened. It takes the Spirit to recognize what the Spirit has done.

How the Spirit Can Work in the Lives of Other

Move beyond manifestations of the Spirit in *your* life. How does the Spirit work among *others*? Recognize the Spirit:

- Wherever someone encounters Christ's call and follows it (John 1:43).
- Wherever presentations of the Word bring greater insights and illumination to someone (Ephesians 1:18).
- Wherever two or three come together in the name of Christ (Matthew 18:20).
- Wherever Christians come together with special energy and sing with gusto and intensity (Colossians 3:16).

- Wherever a follower of Christ finds new levels of joy and peace through release from guilt and expectations of perfection (2 Corinthians 3: 17).
- Wherever a person is considering whether or not to attend church on a Sunday morning and feels the tug to do so (Hebrews 10:25).
- Wherever a fellowship of Christ is experiencing a new heart and a new spirit (Ezekiel 36:26).

Some would understand the "new heart and the new spirit" as a one-time event—at conversion. But understand it as a frequent, even daily process of drowning out the old nature in us through repentance and letting the new nature come forth and arise. Being made new again—renewal—is the Holy Spirit's work (Titus 3: 5). The Spirit's way is movement, not status quo.

Paul explained to the Corinthians that the Holy Spirit transforms us into Christlikeness with the movement of "ever increasing glory" (2 Corinthians 3:18). We are being transformed by the renewing of our minds (Romans 12:2). The Spirit does this with individuals. But he also can do so with congregations. Whatever an individual Christian or a congregation might be reaching for now, there is more the Spirit wants to give and do. Name what he has done so you can recognize what more he can do in the future.

Why Naming the Spirit Is So Important

Founder of the modern discipline of Psychology, William James gave the classic descriptions of religious experiences. He used such phrases as "an incomparable feeling of happiness which is connected with the near presence of God's spirit," and "a sense of presence, strong and at the same time soothing, which hovers over me."

Add to these descriptions from my own survey research of prayer among 500 ordinary Christians. About half said they regularly experience a deep sense of peace and the strong presence of God during prayer. Striking was that about half agreed that "Prayer is the most satisfying experience of my life." Those are experiences of the Holy Spirit, indeed strong experiences. Traditionally, though, we don't associate them with the Holy Spirit. What are some other appropriate phrases for describing the Spirit at work? One is "Spirit encounter." "Spiritual experience" is another, but be sure to capitalize the S. Other good phrases are "a God moment" or "a Spirit sighting."

An "Awakening" is a helpful word for those very special and rare times when one's Christian faith takes on significantly more meaning— when God becomes more real and personal in a new way. It is like an "aha" moment when a light bulb goes on and life in Christ takes on a whole new dimension.

Awakening and Conversion

Such an Awakening is comparable to the Evangelical word "conversion." Evangelicals are taught to recognize such a peak moment and get good at telling their personal conversion story. Sharing these stories helps others review their own conversion and give thanks for God's movement in their lives. One of the limitations of conversion theology, however, is that this special experience happens only once in a lifetime. Often because of a lack of emphasis on the Holy Spirit, those participants are typically not taught to experience additional Spirit-aroused changes on their journey to becoming more like Christ.

In contrast to once-a-lifetime conversion, Luther taught the daily conversion of drowning out the old sinful nature and letting the new nature in Christ emerge. Confession and Absolution are a routine part of weekly worship. Each time is a conversion with a commitment to change that person's mind and amend their life. Both Evangelical believer conversion and Lutheran routine conversion are a story of before and after. As such, they are backwards looking. Indeed, it is good to celebrate renewal that the Spirit has brought in the past. But also important is to look forward to what the Spirit will do in the future. The ministry challenge is to highlight such expectation of fresh movement and more profound conversion to come.

The classical one-time conversion of someone who was not a Christian is a favorite research topic for psychologists. H. Newton Malony concluded that, first, human beings are so constructed that decisions made individually will not last, and second, the confirmation and support of others may be necessary for a conversion to be effective. The first step of naming the Spirit is basic. But it should be followed by sharing the experience not only to confirm it but to describe to others what such an encounter with the Spirit is like, so they can anticipate such movement in their own personal lives.

Gradual Conversion

More recent psychological research on conversion recognizes there is a gradual conversion in addition to the classic sudden and even dramatic conversion. J. T. Richardson suggests this second type is more relational than emotional; it flows from a compassionate rather than stern theology; and it emerges from a search for meaning and purpose. Life-changing conversion to Christian faith does happen to some people at a specific time and place. But for most, it is a process of growth in grace, with perhaps several memorable awakenings along the way.

Psychologist and pastor J. Harold Ellens explains, "The Holy Spirit is always a mystery, an intriguing agent of God, full of intimations of God's nature, truth, and grace. These intimations speak spontaneously to our natures as we hunger for God. One must have the eyes to see and the ears to hear, of course. It is an intriguing and exciting thing indeed to live life always consciously anticipating how the Holy Spirit of God will show up around the next corner. Thy Spirit always does if we are expecting him."

Look for the Spirit in Changed Motivation

An important skill for a sports coach is to motivate players to a higher level of performance. But strictly speaking, no one can motivate someone else. Motives come from within a person and are what move him or her into action. The best someone else can do is to arrange opportunities for a person to fill a need and thus be moved or motivated into action. The opportunity to play first string will stimulate more energy and drive from a bench sitter.

Many participants in churches remain mostly bench sitters. The challenge of ministry is to get them into the "game" of growing more like Christ. How do you do that? We can describe what the new life *should* look like. Call it teaching discipleship. But this approach inherently relies on guilt as the motivator. Guilt, however, is a notoriously poor stimulator of lasting new behavior. The missing ingredient is inner drive. The individual's inner drive has to change. Such a change remains Holy Spirit work.

The modern psychological concept of motivation revolves around filling felt needs. First comes the need that arises from within. This is the inner drive. It initiates a search for ways to fill that need. When a need-filling object is spotted, then comes the action to satisfy it. A late evening craving for a snack arouses someone from the couch to go to the kitchen to find and eat ice cream. This is a simple motivation cycle. Key is to identify the need, the hunger. For believer, the ultimate satisfaction is the abundant life Jesus came to accomplish and that the Holy Spirit offers in the fruit he produces in believers.

Church Motivation

Consider motivation for church behavior. Motivation by guilt is not part of the Gospel of forgiveness in Christ. But in close-knit church communities like those of immigrants, the social pressure could easily become motivation by guilt. For those so motivated, the question too often becomes what is the minimum necessary to do in order to meet those expectations, rather than how to be drawn closer to God.

Psychologists talk about incentives and how to "incentivize" people. The Gospel presents the best possible incentive to act on the filling the highest level of need. Experience the abundant life Jesus came to offer. Experience the fruit of the love, joy and peace the Spirit wants to produce in those who follow Christ. You don't earn these. They are a gift from God empowered by grace through his Spirit.

I have encountered elderly who talk about "paying their dues," as if church is a social club. Indeed, without the strong, continuing work of the Spirit, congregations can become little more than social organizations with a veneer of holy words. The pastoral challenge is to present the Word in ways that more effectively engage the hearers. The difference between an apathetic declining congregation and a lively center of Christian ministry is the Holy Spirit.

Understand the Power of Trigger Events

When I was leading a group on a tour of Israel, we went out on the Sea of Galilee in a tourist boat. We could see many of the special places where Jesus taught and ministered. The operator then played a recording of "How Great Thou Art" at high volume. We sang all three verses—with more and more gusto. In that setting among believers who knew each, our emotions overflowed. The experience blew me away. We were filled with the Spirit and special awe, joy, and unity.

The Spirit works through trigger events, like situations we associate with God. The feeling of awe was aroused by seeing where God walked in the person of Jesus. The feeling of joy came from singing a favorite hymn. The feeling of unity came from a special sense of fellowship with other believers we knew. There was a fourth trigger. The boat was rocking in the water, a mildly unsettling experience. The Spirit often does his work when we are off balance from our usual routines.

How do we know it was the Spirit moving? For us it was in the setting where the Father's love and Christ's grace were evident from Bible stories that happened there. Does it work that way for others? I don't know. But I am certain this was the Spirit moving strongly to shape our feelings.

The Sacraments As Trigger Events

Social psychologists look for events that trigger predictable responses. Marketers fashion words or graphics that trigger a favorable response to their product. Counselors look for events in the past that trigger negative experience a counselee is struggling with. Trigger events can be either good or bad.

In churches rooted in Word and Sacrament ministries, the ultimate positive spiritual trigger event is celebration of the Lord's Supper. In with and under the bread and wine are offered the body and blood of our Savior. That's the event.

I have long been curious about the response of participants returning to their pew. We expect they have a sense of reassurance of their personal relationship with their loving, merciful Father. What other thoughts and feeling might some have? Could sharing such responses improve the experience of others? Comparing experiences can broaden appreciation for how the Spirit can work in participants individually. More discussion of responses could be better stewardship of this basic event.

The other basic sacrament is Baptism. Traditional mainline churches practice infant baptism. Conversion-oriented Evangelical churches expect believer-baptism of those old enough to make their personal confession of faith. Infant-baptism, I think, is superior because it emphasizes that saving faith is granted by God. In his personal struggles Martin Luther would often find comfort in the assurance, I was baptized. What he meant was that God came to me. My relationship with God does not depend on me; it is a gift of God's grace in Christ.

Infant baptism is superior because it embeds faith in the relationships of family and church, who take responsibility to bring up this infant in the faith they have confessed for it. When I was in full-time administration, I would get asked to baptize a child of a colleague. I refused, explaining that this act needs to be done in the context of a congregation that will care for that child.

Consider a new way to improve the trigger event of baptism. Many churches give the family a candle with the encouragement to celebrate annually that baptismal birth. Some families do, but I suspect most don't remember. One practice I have participated in is to have an annual baptismal reaffirmation on the January Sunday marking Jesus's presentation at the Temple. The baptismal font is placed front and center. The invitation is for all who have been baptized to come forward one by one to receive water on their forehead with words like, Remember, you were baptized in the name of the Father, Son and Holy

Spirit. After several services of looking into the eyes and expressions on the face of hundreds of participants, I am always reassured that the Spirit is alive and at work in them.

Additional Means That Can Trigger A Religious Experience

Traditionally, the sacraments of Lord's Supper and Baptism are listed under the Means of Grace. The first is God's Word. The fourth is Confession and Absolution, which has mostly fallen out of use. Martin Luther himself added as a fifth means the Mutual Conversation and Encouragement of Brethren (Smalcald Articles, Part III, Article IV). This fifth means never got much traction in traditional practice. Small group ministries today are a good application. The writer of Hebrews challenges us to "consider how we may spur one another on toward love and good deeds. Let us encourage one another."

Traditional churches have relied on triggers for *transcendent* experiences, meaning above and beyond the ordinary. They meet in settings very different from weekday environments. Worship happens in sanctuaries with stained glass windows and is done with organ music, now associated only with churches. Sunday is meant to be a weekly uplifting experience. Transcendent worship is "formal." These are highly structured triggers.

Younger Christians today look for *immanent* experiences closely related to their normal daily life. They respond to different triggers. They are comfortable meeting in buildings that have other uses, like a gym or mall. Clothing is casual, including that of the leaders. Music is with guitars and drums, much like what they hear in popular contemporary music. "Informal" is a very appropriate summary of the immanent style.

Traditional transcendent triggers do not work for everyone. For many, those cues from childhood bring negative associations of boredom or oppressive guilt. They don't work either for someone who has never been in a sanctuary. Many young adults are out there whose only exposure to a sanctuary is perhaps involvement in a wedding, now just one of many other novel settings for the nuptials.

Two Church Cultures

Theologian John Shea observed that Church and Tradition enshrined a set of triggers. The problem is these are being questioned today. "The presence that people used to find in the dark back of Gothic churches they now claim to find in the bright light of the secular world."

He describes how today the more-traveled path to having religious experiences is found in the multiple life situations in which people find themselves—of sickness and vitality, of questing for truth and struggling for justice, of loving and reconciling.

Transcendent church and Immanent church are two different cultures. Most community churches start with Immanent church. "Non-denominational" is their code word to communicant this. The roots of traditional churches are in the now old-fashioned Transcendent culture.

These two approaches to church life often conflict in a congregation that offers both styles, even when the sanctuary service continues as it was. These are different church cultures. It's like learning a new language. It is indeed a new and different culture with different triggers.

Whispers From The Spirit

Have you ever had notion pop into your head that you should go and visit someone? Could the Holy Spirit be planting that whisper?

I experienced a loud whisper from the Spirit in work with our sister church body in Haiti. On a trip to a church site damaged by an earthquake, we were envisioning how much better the work of ministering to others and building new houses would go if we had a guest house for visiting teams. I can remember exactly where I was standing when I had this strong urge to pay a significant amount of money to buy property for this guesthouse. The whisper said to talk to a specific woman in our group. So I asked if she would put down the same amount. It was a short exchange: if you do, I will. We did. That initial investment proved crucial in carrying momentum for ministries that flourished from this base.

At Jesus' baptism in the River Jordon, he came up out of the water and saw a dove descending from heaven and alighting on him. Focus on the image of that dove as the Third Person of the Trinity, the Holy Spirit. Now imagine that dove sitting on your shoulder whispering silently into your ear. In workshops, that biblical image has proven very productive for many. To complete it, you have to also imagine the Enemy sitting on your other shoulder whispering thoughts that lead you astray. Which voice will you pay attention to?

I vividly recall a personal encounter with the Spirit when I felt a calling January 15, 1990 to plant a church and move the family cross country. That kind of personal experience is basic to the traditional understanding of a calling to a specific ministry. Recalling such a loud, convicting whisper is so valuable when encountering discouraging difficulties, especially starting a new church. Remembering this whisper experience reaffirms that this is God's doing, not just my own.

Whisper Stories

In workshops I have done, almost every small group has a person with a whisper story to tell. All listen carefully. One was by a woman coming home from shopping who felt an urge to visit a friend she had not seen in a while. It turns out that woman was baking and needed eggs, which this visitor could provide. That exchange led into a God-focused lengthy discussion of issues they were dealing with. I believe that whisper was the Spirit at work.

In my first workshop on the Holy Spirit, a participant shared a whisper story and was relieved to understand it could be a word from God. He had thought there was something wrong with him. For traditional believers, the realization that God is reaching out to them personally here and now opens up a whole new relationship with God. We were taught that God did mighty things in biblical times, and he talked to specific people. But we weren't led to the understanding that God wants to talk with his followers now, just like he did then. Whisper stories add new meaning to Paul's encouragement that we stay in step with the Spirit in our daily living.

Cautions

Of course, we need to be sure that this is the Spirit at work and not just some personal idea that comes to mind. The basic test is whether this whisper advocates God-pleasing behavior. The Spirit will never prompt what is counter to God's love and mercy. If the whisper suggests a major personal decision, wisdom lies in the direction of consulting with a few other mature Christians to get their perspective.

Martin Luther learned to be cautious dealing with Enthusiasts who concluded that the Holy Spirit was calling them to rebel against the civil authorities. They led what is called the Peasants' Revolt of 1525. The sad result was the slaughter of hundreds of thousands. Theirs was not God-pleasing action. That was not the Holy Spirit leading them on.

Christ's Spirit is God's empowering presence. Scripture teaches that the Spirit unleashes real life-changing power, not just some vague spiritual feelings. That's why care must always be practiced when invoking the Spirit's presence and power. Recognize that the Spirit brings clarity, not confusion. It helps to distinguish between the Spirit working in my personal life and the Spirit being wished upon others.

For personal applications, be sure to seek the advice of others. That's why Luther recognized the mutual conversation and encouragement of fellow believers to be the fifth means of God's grace. When encountering others who are advocating the Spirit's power for specifics in your life, be cautious. Be doubly cautious about invoking what the Spirit wants in the personal behaviors of others.

Test Those Who Speak in the Name of the Spirit

The first of the four Great Awakenings in American history happened in the 1730s and 40s. Arguably American's greatest theologian, Jonathan Edwards was involved but grew skeptical as the Awakening worked its way out.

That movement brought great controversy. One side emphasized religious emotions as the essence; feeling the love of God was most important. The other side taught that the heart of true religion is right thinking; emotions are fickle and often lead astray.

Edwards was decidedly Word-oriented. In his writings he argued against a shallow, human-oriented view of spirituality. He taught to look for the following signs of the Spirit's indwelling.

Does the presenter have a new spiritual sense and conviction that does not come from self-interest? Check on the wealth of the featured speaker/healer. Evidence of self-interest should raise doubt about the Spirit's dominance.

Is there a pervasive sense of humility? When the Spirit is at work, he changes hearts to bring a new humility. The Spirit cannot do much with a person who is full of him or herself. Be cautious with someone whose personal life does not reflect a Christ-like Spirit. Do they practice what they preach?

Since "emotions" can be a highly charged word in traditional ministry practices, we do better to talk about "affections." Edwards defined affections as strong inclinations of the soul that are manifested in thinking, feeling and acting. Affection includes a belief held with strong conviction.

Affections can be either good or bad. The difference is the good lead us toward God and the bad away from God. According to Edwards, questionable affections often go along with prideful, show-off quoting of many Scripture passages or self-serving eloquent talk, or passionate praise for God, or pharisaical devotion to religious activities.

Consider this perspective of Martin Luther. According to scholar Simeon Zahl, "affections" and the heart were at the center of Luther's theology of justification and sanctification. For Luther, right motivation and willingness of the heart were far more important before God than right action. Luther recognized that our affections are indeed transformed by the Spirit of God.

Getting the Theology of the Spirit Right

1054 A.D. was a significant milestone in the history of the Christian church. That's when the split occurred between the Latin-speaking Western church and the Greek-speaking Eastern church. Does the Third Person Holy Spirit proceed from the First-Person Father alone or also from the Second-Person Son Jesus Christ? That "also from the Son" in the Latin phrase is "filioque." This is known as the filioque controversy.

The issue is very relevant to our understanding how the Spirit works in our lives today. The Greek original word for the Holy Spirit is Paraclete, one who comes alongside, like a lawyer who advocates the case of his client. The client is God. The Spirit advocates for the will of the Father and the Son in our personal lives. He manifests himself in people's lives through working out the love of the Father and applying the grace offered in Jesus Christ. He will not advocate what is contrary to God's Word.

The Holy Spirit is Christ's Spirit, as Paul explicitly identifies him. In his letters, Christ's Spirit and the Holy Spirit are interchangeable. They are like a two-sided coin. Jesus Christ did his redemptive work 2,000 years ago. Ascended, he is now present with us through his Spirit.

Jesus' Teaching

Let Jesus himself clarify this theology as he explained the basics to Nicodemus in John 3. "No one can see the kingdom of God unless he is born again. Flesh gives birth to flesh, but the Spirit gives birth to human spirit."

The Greek for born again really means born from on high. Being a born-again Christians is a favorite phrase among Evangelicals. We can and should celebrate the Spirit's movement in the heart and mind of any believer. Jesus clarifies that no one can enter the kingdom of God unless he is born of water and the Spirit. We traditional Protestants believe that happens in infant baptism, which is entry into the family of God. The liturgical phrase is that the Father has given the "new birth of water and of the Spirit."

The second part of Jesus' teaching is that Spirit "gives birth" to spirit. That phrase is hard to translate in this context. A second dictionary definition would render the Spirit *influences* human spirit, like a teacher influences his students. Human spirit is one of the words the Bible uses for "soul" or "heart" or "inner being." A modern equivalent is "motivation." The Spirit can and will change the motivations of those who are open to him.

Jesus also taught Nicodemus, "The wind blows wherever it pleases. You hear its sound, but you cannot tell where it comes from or where it is going. So it is with everyone born of the Spirit." What are we to make out of the Spirit who blows where he will? That's the puzzle and challenge of ministry in traditional churches that once had spiritually robust church life and now are but a shadow of what they were. What happened to the Spirit?

The Miraculous in the Spirit's Work

What's revolutionary is to recognize that the supernatural can intervene in the natural. How this happens touches on the miraculous, an extraordinary event for which there is no natural explanation. Traditional Protestants were taught this does not happen anymore after New Testament times. The result is an anemic view of the Spirit today. Better theology that includes God's miraculous acts today points to a much more robust understanding of the Spirit at work in our midst now.

The logic is simple. Christ ascended and left his Spirit behind to do his work while he is with his Father in authority. We believers are challenged to become sanctified, to become more like Christ in our daily living. Christ's Spirit empowers us to do that. Christ's Spirit changes our motivations so that we behave in new Christ-like ways. Jesus came that we may have the abundant life now. The Holy Spirit produces fruit like love, joy, and peace that make up the abundant life here in this world. This is the ministry message.

Pentecost was a peak time when God's empowering presence made itself felt and the Gospel was proclaimed in truly dynamic ways. Does the Spirit usually work this way? No, most of the time this Spiritual engine is idling in the lives of Christ's followers. But then in certain places at certain times, this engine revs up. It happens in special personal Awakenings and Spiritual encounters. At a church level, I think this is what's happening among certain Bible-focused community churches that become recognized as "happening" places?

Peter's message on Pentecost started with Joel's prophecy that God "will pour out my Spirit on all people." Couple that image of "pouring out" with a jar being filled with water. Sometimes the jar is full to overflowing. But we all have a hole in our personal jar. It's called sin. Our sinful nature opposes the things of God and robs us of the Spirit's power to transform our lives. How can our jar get filled again? It has to begin with a fresh encounter with God's Word and recognizing evidence of the Spirit currently at work in us personally and among fellow believers. That's the value of learning to name the Spirit touching lives in and around us today.

Focus On The Spirit Alive Today

Theologian John Shea describes Christians as people of Memory and the Spirit. He notes that this living relationship produces many outward forms for expressing and sustaining that relationship. These include many rituals, elaborated beliefs, theologies, espoused values and behavior. But as generation succeeds generation, these trigger words and rituals lose their impact and recede into shared memory. Some congregations do indeed seem to exist mostly as a museum without much evidence of a current living relationship with God. John Shea explains that these rituals and formulations are in constant need of refreshment and reform in order to be faithful to the living God they want to reflect.

Do the people of a withering congregation still have a living relationship with God today? Or are they trying to carry forward memories of what used to be? How do you recognize when a "living relationship with God" is mostly gone?

The Spirit is present where God's Word is at work. But his impact may be limited when he is expected to work only through old forms and formulations that don't communicate well to new generations. Almost certainly a living relationship has weakened when believers no longer express excitement about future opportunities to share God's love and when they no longer find the energy to do so.

In John Shea's words, "When we retain the message of the King but lose the feel for his presence, the passion of religious mission turns to dull obligation."

Encourage Others by Sharing Experiences Of The Spirit

Name the Spirit is the first step in re-energizing personal and congregational spiritual life. The second is to **Share** such Spiritual experiences for mutual encouragement. The third will be commitment to **Seek More** such experiences through practices that the Spirit can use to draw followers closer to Christ.

"The Mutual Conversation and Encouragement of Brethren"

Martin Luther understood the importance of encouraging by sharing experiences. He had many friends and colleagues in Wittenberg. As the Reformation took off, his Augustinian order disbanded and gave their monastery building to Luther. Soon he headed a growing family. The former monk cells were rented out as a dormitory to university students. All shared the big meal of the day, along with colleagues who would stop by, like his friend Philip Melanchthon. Luther was a natural storyteller, and he would share his personal experiences to enlivened whatever topic they were discussing. Students recorded those lively conversations in 31 volumes of Table Talks.

Those fond memories led Martin Luther to include in the Smalcald Articles of 1537 what was never really noted or appreciated in the following heritage. In the article on the Gospel he listed five means of grace. The fifth is the Mutual Conversation and Encouragement of Brethren (Part III, Article IV). The first three Means are the Word, the Lord's Supper and Baptism. The fourth one has slipped out of use, the Power of the Keys (Confession and Absolution).

Strictly speaking, mutual encouragement does not belong in this listing. We believe the Word, Baptism and the Lord's Supper offer, convey, and seal God's promises in the Gospel of grace. This mutual encouragement does not appear as a means of grace in other confessional writings. What we can confidently conclude, though, is that such encouragement was very important to Martin Luther personally. He wrote the Smalcald Articles himself.

Paul on Encouragement

Mutual encouragement was highly valued by the Apostle Paul, too. He urged the Thessalonians, "Therefore encourage one another and build each other up, just as in fact you are doing."

After he and Silas were released from prison in Philippi, they met with others at Lydia's house, where he encouraged them and received their comfort and encouragement in return. We know he was thankful to the Philippians for the care they gave him, and he sent his colleague Tychicus to encourage them.

The writer of the letter to Hebrews (traditionally thought to be Paul) encouraged that we "not give up meeting together but let us encourage one another."

Paul ends his second letter to the Thessalonians with a string of encouragements. First, they should encourage each other with his teaching about the second coming of the Lord. Encourage the timid, help the weak, be patient with everyone, be joyful, pray continually, give thanks. Then he associates such encouragement with the Spirit's fire. Do not put it out. We can note that the same Greek word for encouragement is also used for the Holy Spirit—the paraclete who comes by your side to advocate and comfort. Christ's Spirit is the Great Encourager. Moved by the Spirit, we can be encouragers, too.

Encouraged by the Evidence

Evidenced-based practices in health care and education have become a new emphasis in those fields. Key is statistical research on the experience of those who have received certain kinds of treatment or were taught with different approaches. How many patients got better? How much did children learn from one grade to the next? This information is then combined with the practitioner's clinical experience to determine best practices for bringing better results.

The Apostle Paul took an evidence-based approach to developing a new kind of community with shared experiences. These were all first-generation followers of Christ who had first-hand experience of the Spirit working in their lives. They shared the Spiritual experience of becoming a distinctive fellowship called out to become more like Christ in their life together. They each showed evidence of the Spirit working in and through them. In his encouragement Paul relied on such evidence of lives changed.

In writing to the troubled Corinthians, Paul reviewed how they came to faith. "I came to you in weakness and fear, and with much trembling. My message and my preaching were not with wise and persuasive words, but with a demonstration of the Spirit's power, so that your faith might not rest on men's wisdom, but on God's power." To the Romans, he declared simply, The Spirit lives in you and makes you sons of God.

Without consciousness of the Spirit's power, so much Christian preaching winds up relying mostly on wise and persuasive words. So long as the Word of God is presented, the Spirit can do his work. But why not add evidence of the power of the Spirit in lives changed here and now, preferably among those who are gathered? That's what Paul did.

Certainly, the objective facts of salvation in Christ's redemptive work need to be kept clearly in focus. But subjective evidence adds persuasiveness. So long as the subjective never replaces or substitutes for the objective, why not lift up and share evidence of the Spirit's power available today, not just in biblical times? It is those stories that can increase the encouragement shared among those gathered around God's Word.

The Fruit of the Spirit

The evidence for the worth of a fruit tree is the fruit it bears. Jesus used that analogy in his teaching on the vine, branches and much fruit. Paul makes it foundational for his theology of the Christ's Spirit, as he listed for the Galatians the fruit the Spirit produces: love, joy, peace, patience, kindness, goodness, faithfulness, gentleness and self-control. You don't have to look far for evidence of the Spirit's power in individual lives. It's there in the feelings he generates in individual believers. Has someone experienced unusual joy in their Christian walk? Share it. Has someone experienced an extra degree of patience? Such stories of the Spirit's fruit are always good to offer as encouragement to others. Especially helpful are stories of gaining self-control in relation to others. We can work those into mutual conversation and encouragement.

The Christian church has a long tradition of interpreting Paul's fruit as human virtues to be pursued. The roots go back to the Greek philosopher Aristotle. But with that mindset, we are left with only wise and persuasive words to make a difference in followers of Christ. Virtue is then something we need to pursue on our own strength.

Paul is the Apostle of grace as God's gift to us in Christ. He understood grace to extend to God's gift of the Spirit who changes lives. We are not left on our own to pursue a godly life. God gives those basic qualities as the work of the Spirit. Jesus did not leave us as orphans. He gave us his Spirit. Look for and share evidence of his work. That's a good way to re-energize Spiritual life.

Develop A Church Culture That Affirms the Spirit

The poet T. S. Eliot famously observed, "We had the experience but missed the meaning." All practicing Christians have had experiences of the Spirit. Most Christians in traditional churches weren't taught the meaning.

That's because we were taught to look for statements or propositions of truth in doctrinal language, like "God is love." Yes, but what does that look like? The traditional Protestants I know weren't taught to look for evidence of the Spirit's work in their personal lives. They don't think they have anything significant to share. We joyfully retell the evidence in the Bible and affirm the truths basic to living the life God intends for us. We affirm that the Gospel "works." But we don't share much evidence of lives actually changed in our times.

Telling Stories

John Shea is a storyteller and theologian who wrote *An Experience Named Spirit*. His book was very challenging for me because he mostly just tells stories. I am used to looking for greater truths and generalizations. But that is his point. "Storytelling has a power of involvement and appreciation that the mere noting of patterns or talking about experiences analytically does not have."

In greeting visitors, a community church near me stresses, We want to hear your story. That seems a bit forward for us older folk. But it seems to work for younger adults. Their story usually has something to do with a hurt, a lack of meaning in life or a longing for community. Such stories naturally lead to a response of how the greeter found greater meaning or security. It is then up to biblically based, Gospel-oriented pastors to give fuller explanation to the faith that is displayed. The challenge is to test the spirits and keep the focus on Christ.

Withering traditional churches are in need of renewal. Where better to look than the first churches. Scholar Gordon F. Fee wrote, "It is certain that Pauline churches were 'charismatic' in the sense that the dynamic presence of the Spirit was manifested in their gatherings. Paul recognizes a miraculous work of the Spirit that was evidenced by the way renewed people behave towards one another. Whatever else, the Spirit was experienced in the Pauline churches; the Spirit was not merely a matter of creedal assent."

We can aim to help withering churches today move beyond just creedal assent to the Spirit. We can share when we experienced new levels of the Spirit's fruit like love, joy, peace patience and self-control. Many traditional Protestants may be reluctant to take such initiative, assuming what happened is too personal or not important. Or they may fear rejection in some form. But find the courage to share stories of your own God-moments with others. Do it for their sake! The Spirit moving in you can move in others, too.

Moving Beyond a Village Culture

To understand the traditional reluctance to share personal experiences, go back to the formative social setting where mainline churches thrived in previous centuries. These were mostly small villages where roughly eighty percent of a country's population lived, usually in clusters of fifty or so families in proximity to their farmland. Such villages dominated American life well into the 20th century. Among immigrants to this country, village-like neighborhoods and mentality continued in big cities as well.

One village reality is that you do not want to draw attention to yourself. Everyone has to get along with each other, and that is easier to do when you don't think of yourself as better than others. An old adage is the nail that sticks its head up will get pounded down.

Villagers who seem especially pious make others uncomfortable. Village churches teach "closet" prayer, based on Matthew 6: 6. "But when you pray, go into your room and shut the door and pray to your Father who is in secret. And your Father who sees in secret will reward you." Prayer was not something you shared with someone else. Prayer was done by the pastor, usually at the altar, and then mostly only for someone who was sick. In this setting, personalized spiritual growth was not important and even resisted.

When I did a major research project on prayer practices and experiences of ordinary Lutherans, I was surprised to discover that half said their personal prayers were the most satisfying experience they had. You would never know that from observance of routine church life.

Don't Settle For A Church Cultural With Only Minimal Spiritual Encouragement

One of my peeves in my church experience is how little spiritual encouragement goes on beyond the worship service itself. Conversations tend to be ordinary small talk about what the children are doing or the latest in sports. Visiting Evangelical churches, I would listen in on conversations after the service and hear greetings like, What's God doing in your life? Or, how can I pray for you? When I became part of the Evangelical community of Fuller Theological Seminary, in the first months I was prayed for by name more than in all my previous years of church life. Such personalized spiritual attention makes for an attractive community.

Village preachers had a captive audience. Their job was to raise up children in the faith, which meant training them in the dry impersonal propositions of the catechism. University educated, they typically presented sermons as lectures with little application to daily living. Personal spiritual growth was not on the academic agenda. Those who attended weekly worship typically were reacting to strong social pressure to do so. A favorite story for me is how a village rector thought fathers should be present for the baptism of their child, and if absent the pastor would send out the police to bring him in. Imagine what such coerced attendance of a captive audience did for the dynamics of church life.

Openness to "outsiders" is not characteristic of that old heritage. No outsiders exist in a village setting, where, by definition, everybody is an insider. Now, of course, we live in a world where ethnic heritages are fast fading. Do we blindly go forward with our culture and become like a museum? Or, while we continue to treasure the biblical Gospel that is the core of the heritage, do we look for ways to improve a supportive church culture welcoming those who do not know the traditions.

Opt for the latter kind of church. Be willing to go beyond your comfort zone to be a church where everybody is welcome to learn the Good News in Christ with as few barriers as possible. Learn that Christ is present with us now through his Holy Spirit and that this Spirit works on hearts as well as heads. Name the Spirit in your church life. Share your experiences with each other.

Everybody can learn to be an encourager in Christ, like Paul. For the sake of the Gospel, try it.

Newer Approaches to Building Up Fellowships of the Holy Spirit

The answer to what is a "fellowship of the Spirit" was easy in Paul's times. Believers met together weekly in house churches, which could accommodate perhaps about thirty or forty people. The number was small enough that everyone could know each other, their background stories, their struggles and their hopes.

Fellowship, or *koinonia* in the original, means literally to share something with someone. Today we have gotten used to mostly symbolic fellowship. We share a building, an assembly at a worship service. Our offerings support a shared pastor and paid staff. But most participants typically don't know the background story and struggles of more than a dozen or so fellow members.

Small Groups

The ideal setting for the Spirit to work in the lives of Christ followers is that of believers gathered around God's Word and sharing its application in their lives. This can happen through preaching in a worship service, but the applications typically don't get personal. To provide more fellowship was the promise of the small group movement that gained prominence in recent decades. Typical first efforts divided the congregation by geographic area and encouraged neighbors to gather at someone's home. But such groupings did not last long. There needs to be some other common interest to provide the glue that holds a small group together over time.

I have been leading and promoting small group ministries for more than thirty years. It has been an uphill struggle all the way. The best we've done is get penetration of only about five percent of the congregation' total adult membership. We do hear stories of some congregations that have flourishing small group programs. Typically, they are in new suburbs with new residents looking for social relationships.

Following Covid, some small groups have found value in continuing to meet virtually over Zoom. This can be especially valuable for those who have children at home and can schedule an hour without blocking out the whole evening. Evolving technology opens up new possibilities for those who have the leadership skills to shape new program formats.

Finding Others with Similar Spiritual Temperaments

Congregations can help members find others they can more readily bond with. One approach is to identify those who share a spiritual temperament. Such a temperament is the way each of us personally relates to God best and most naturally. Spiritual temperaments influence where and how we most often sense God speaking to us, refreshing us, and stirring our passion for Him.

At church we have some members who seek out those needing special care, especially when in wheelchairs. Praise God for those who share the temperament of caregivers. This is a form of pastoral care, considered basic to professional ministry. I have had training and know what to do. But I don't jump at opportunities. My spiritual temperament is different.

Gary Thomas in *Sacred Pathways: Discover Your Soul's Pathway to God* has done the most helpful work on identifying differing spiritual temperaments. There is no right or wrong temperament. These are givens in your personality. He offers an inventory of questions helpful to identify your own main pathways. Seven such temperaments are:

The *Naturalist*: Loving God Out-of-Doors. Finds a walk through the woods to be very conducive to prayer.

The *Sensate*: Loving God with the Senses. Wants to be lost in awe, beauty, and splendor of God.

The *Traditionalist*: Loving God through Ritual and Symbol. Likes structured worship with symbols and sacraments.

The *Activist*: Loving God through Confrontation. Serves a God of justice, and church life recharges batteries.

The *Caregiver*: Loving God by Loving Others. Serves God by serving others.

The *Enthusiast*: Loving God with Mystery and Celebration. Wants to be inspired by joyful celebration.

The *Intellectual*: Loving God with the Mind. Drawn to explore basic issues in theology and church life.

How Differing Temperaments Express Themselves

Over the centuries, believers have found ways to be with others of like temperament. *Naturalists* have been drawn to thirteenth-century Francis of Assisi, and this monastic order is still the most popular. *Sensates* gravitate toward others who feel special connection with God through the arts and music.

When describing *Activists,* Gary Thomas had in mind social activists who feel a calling to pursue peace and justice in society, which is a form of piety in many mainline church bodies. That temperament can also include leaders, like me, who are inclined to test out where the Spirit is leading by putting ideas into action and watching for results.

Traditionalists like the assurance that they are approaching God through symbols and formats that have been used for generations. Assurance of continuity with the saints can be very helpful--until it turns into traditionalism that blocks new movements of the Spirit.

Traditional churches have a heritage of leadership by *Intellectuals,* who like to explore in depth various shades of differences in understanding the Bible and teachings derived from it. Intellectuals typically have low tolerance for Enthusiasts. One reading of American church history is that those with an Enthusiast temperament broke free from Intellectually dominated mainline churches to form their own church bodies with their own church culture and resources, like Pentecostals today. Can old-line denominations become more welcoming to Enthusiasts?

Accommodating Differing Spiritual Temperaments

Over time believers will sort themselves out to be with others who share their spiritual temperament. That's what's happening, I believe, with the non-denominational community church movement gaining momentum in the suburbs. Young families like to be with others who share the same middle-class hopes and stresses and who like easily accessible insights from an authoritative source on how to raise their families and find fulfillment in their lives. The Bible can provide that.

Large congregations have the option to increase their attractiveness by offering a variety of ministries that appeal to different spiritual temperaments. That's what is happening with churches that develop a contemporary worship alternative to the formal liturgy that is so appealing to Traditionalists.

Small congregations typically become niche churches appealing to a small segment of the population. Try to avoid becoming trapped into appealing to only one temperament. Ultimately, the Holy Spirit is the one doing the calling into a specific fellowship of believers. Follow his lead with the specific people he sends. Strive to accommodate at least several spiritual temperaments with creative ministries.

Stories of Spiritual Experiences

James Loder had a transforming moment early in his career as a professor at Princeton Seminary. He spent the rest of his academic career explaining it in biblical and psychological terms.

His moment came September 2, 1970, traveling to Canada for a family vacation. He saw a woman standing on the roadside near a disabled car and stopped to help. Just as he had his head under the fender trying to change a tire, this car was hit from behind by a driver who had fallen asleep behind the wheel. Loder explained his reaction in *The Transforming Moment*.

"As I roused myself from under the car, a steady surge of life was rushing through me. I never felt more conscious of the life that poured through me, nor more aware that this life was not my own. My well-being came from beyond my natural strength. By far, the most significant memorable effect was not the pain, nor the anger, but the gracious nature of the life I was experiencing. My sense was that the power was emanating from the center of Another's awareness—an awareness that positively, even joyfully intended my well-being."

James Loder offers a number of observations about such specific experiences. He became conversant with the theories of psychologists about this kind of peak experience. While thy can describe and classify various such events, they cannot explain the content . There is no way to validate as truth such an impression of life beyond the ordinary. It is finally the person with such experiences who has to determine it to be authoritative for how he or she lives in the future.

David S. Luecke

Theological Repression of Spiritual Experiences

Loder writes about "theological repression" of these convictional experiences. They are too subjective to fit into the rigorous demands of theological thinking, and too unique to be coped with by highly generalized theological systems. Academic theology is the wrong place to look. A better source is the story language of personal convictions of individuals.

Consider Loder's conclusion: "The effect of this repression is manifested, for example, within the United Presbyterian Church U.S.A., a mainline denomination of which I am a member. It stresses theology, a cognitive, confessional orientation to faith that is basic to academically trained clergy. As a result, it generally appeals to the middle and upper social strata of society. An open conversation about convicting experiences and their significance for life and faith is the exception among Presbyterians.

"Yet a recent survey showed that 80 percent of our clergy and approximately half of our lay constituency have had such experiences. The theological repression of such experiences has generated a deep, untapped, convictional unconscious among Presbyterians and, on the basis of other research, I would suspect among other churches as well."

What Loder says about Presbyterians I know to be true of Lutherans, based on my own research and on dozens of workshops I led.

Surely the way forward for withering mainline church bodies is to have participants share their stories of personal conviction and how the work of Christ's Spirit affects the way they live.

A Story About Storms and Flying Like An Eagle

"I am not sure that I am in the eye of the storm now and will see the storm winds of cancer begin to howl again, or if I am coming out of this storm altogether. We all face storms in our lives, and it is amazing that God uses those storms to bring us closer to him."

So writes Jeff, a member of our congregation who fought cancer for four years and is now in remission. He shared his observations on a website for the caring community.

"If you are flying like an eagle, thank God for today and the blessing that it is. If you are in a storm now, understand that God stands with you today to brace against the winds for you and to love you unconditionally, and that now is the time you will become closer to God. Give thanks for that."

Do you, the reader, find these words encouraging? I do, and I think this is a great example of a Christian fellowship at work. Here is the mutual conversation and encouragement that Martin Luther considered to be so important.

Note Jeff's twice-made observation that he was drawn closer to God through his personal storm. What does such closeness look and feel like? In other entries over the years, he described his thankfulness for care providers, his heightened appreciation for the gift of life, his renewed sense of love for family and friends, his sense of peace during the howling storm.

Finding and Telling Current Faith Stories

Fellowship means sharing something with somebody. The Spirit does his work through a community of believers sharing insights from God's Word. Bible promises are basic. How those promises are experienced by other believers adds persuasiveness. Centuries-old churches have a long tradition of spiritual matters being handled only by the pastor, who typically relies on Bible promises to offer consolation. Concerned with confidentiality, pastors typically don't tell stories about the personal spiritual experiences and struggles of others. They can, however, ask permission to share highlights. In my experience most are willing to give this.

Personal faith stories can get long and complicated. The attention span of those hearing or reading such an account is limited. How can a fellowship make faith-affirming stories of its members easily available to others? Digital technology opens up new possibilities. Such testimonies can be recorded on video and then edited to make the story more succinct. A four-minute story can be shown in a worship service and placed on the church website.

The work of editing and offering succinctly told personal faith stories is time consuming. Who will do that? Large churches can make this a staff assignment, but that requires commitment to the priority of sharing God-moments. Pray for a member of the fellowship to catch the vision of committing their personal time to this new form of ministry. Add to the Spirit-gifted ministries of 1 Corinthians 12 that of videographer.

Cautions

"Spiritual experience" is a very broad category. I am using it here to mean a person's experiences of the Holy Spirit at work in his or her life. How do you know if it is truly the divine Spirit or simply reflections of human spirit on lofty things? The difference is whether the experience points to Christ as the center of a believer's relationship with God. The Holy Spirit advocates Christ-like living with more of the Spirit's fruit of love, joy, peace patience and other feelings.

Clearly the focus on feelings can go too far when it loses sight of objective facts that shape who we are. But I see myself addressing a traditional church culture that is out of balance toward the objective side. Dale Carnegie's classic book *How the Win Friends and Influence People* had a big influence on my younger self. The basic principle to winning friends is to get them to talk about themselves. Offer encouragement. Then work to build that relationship into greater appreciation for biblical living.

The Apostle John warned to test the spirits. Do they glorify Christ? If so, that's worth hearing about.

Seek **GROWTH** in the Spirit's Influence

Growing In The Benefits The Spirit Offers

The Great Passion by James Runcie is a novel about the family and work of J.S. Bach set in the 1730s. He was the hard-working organist and music director at St. Thomas Church in Leipzig, Germany and is now recognized as one of the greatest composers of all times. Striking in the novel was his busy household of 20 children, nine of whom died in childhood.

I read the novel as a reflection of the German church culture of the 18th century, aspects of which continued well into the 20th century. In one's personal life, the emphasis was on work and discipline, and the solution to most problems was to work harder. Suffering was a constant, especially with illness and death so near at hand. With suffering came an emphasis on heaven; relief will come in the next life. Individuality was to be resisted. Identity was to be determined through church life and routines. Overall, life was somber.

I bring to this older culture a distinction between a static view of church life and a dynamic approach that is replacing it. *Static* is like a flat line. You did your growing as a child. As an adult, you do your work until you are called home. Your church life supported you over the years as you tried to live a virtuous, disciplined life. The opposite of static is *dynamic*—frequently changing. Personal life has its downturns, but more important is change upward through growth of some sort. Personal growth in our current culture is increasingly seen as a life-long process.

This distinction between static and dynamic is over simplified to make the point that personal spiritual growth toward closeness to God was not emphasized in earlier centuries of church life. More important was maintaining the faith you were taught while you encountered difficulties in your life.

The six Reflections that follow assume a Spirit-stimulated personal drive to become more like Christ. You become different over time. What does such growth look like? What can you do to better position yourself so the Spirit can change your life?

Growing in Faith

My first effort as a spiritual director was with a student who wanted to grow in his faith. I did not know how to respond and help. That's because I was coming out of a static church culture. My understanding of faith was a set of beliefs that I held as I went through my family and work life. Any growth would be in knowledge about God and what he expects of those who follow him.

Since that encounter, I have grown into a broader understanding of faith in a believer's life. It can be either a noun or a verb. My assumption was that faith is a noun, something I believe. I have learned to see it more as a verb, something I do. The same biblical word can mean both. The action verb is to trust. The challenge in Christian living is to grow in trusting God in a relationship that deepens and brings more benefits in the abundant life Jesus came to offer.

To appreciate that abundant life, you have to think like Paul and recognize the Spirit as the giver of benefits when we experience more of his fruit of love, joy, peace, patience, kindness, goodness, faithfulness, gentleness and self-control. The Spirit is dynamic. He wants to bring change into those who follow Christ. The question I will address in the next six Reflections is, What can we ourselves do to let the Spirit draw us closer to him?

Growing in Grace[2]

The Apostle Peter challenged his readers to "grow in grace and knowledge" (2 Peter 3:18). I know how to grow in knowledge. I have been doing that all my life. But how do you grow in grace?

The problem goes back to the static view of life with God that does not anticipate continued growth. Your faith in the Gospel of Christ puts you in a new saved relationship with God. You live that life as best you can until you are with God in eternal life. By grace are you saved by faith; it is the gift of God.

But this static approach of new standing before God misses the dynamic view of grace that Paul developed. The whole concept of grace is unique to Paul. The parallel term used by Jesus in the Gospels is mercy, which Paul amplified. We can speculate that Paul developed the basics of his new theology during his fourteen silent years (Galatians 2: 1) while he witnessed to his Greek neighbors around Tarsus. They were steeped in the mythology of major and minor gods. Among the minor ones were the Charity Sisters, who were viewed as muses, or the source for ideas for poetry and dance. What the muses inspired was offered as a gift, and we get the English word "charity" as the giving of gifts to others. Paul emphasized the word *charis* to describe the gift of our new status before God. But the Greeks would have heard it also in the dynamic terms of new powers we receive from God. That is described with the word *charisma*, from which we get the word charismatic.

For clarity between the static view of *charis* and the dynamic understanding of *charisma*, I suggest the labels of Grace¹ and Grace². These modern terms can be helpful to highlight the subtle distinction Paul made in describing two kinds of gifts from God. Grace¹ (*charis*) is the status of salvation in Christ. Grace² (*charisma*) is best described by Paul in 1 Corinthians 12, where he clarifies spiritual giftings to do ministry. For Paul, everyone is given a dynamic manifestation of the Spirit for the common good. Ministry is done by all. This is a radical shift in perspective that is fundamental to the view of congregational ministry I am trying to highlight. It is so Scriptural and so powerful.

The Greater Gifts

But perhaps even more significant and powerful is the last verse of that chapter where Paul introduces "the greater gifts." The first example is love, so eloquently described in 1 Corinthians 13 and then combined with faith and hope. He expands that listing in Galatian 5 to include joy, peace, patience, and five other qualities. He calls these "fruit" of the Spirit—what the Spirit produces in the lives where he is active.

What are these fruit of the Spirit? For centuries they were regarded as virtues, qualities that describe a life well lived. The understanding from ancient times is that an individual should strive to achieve these virtues. Church life and preaching too often held up this understanding of a standard that we should aim to attain. But to achieve a virtuous life is to submit to a stern taskmaster.

What if, however, these qualities are the product of the Spirit's work? What if they are Grace[2] given freely? Paul's fruit of the Spirit are all personal qualities everyone would like to have more of in their lives. Being closer to God is not something we are left on our own to achieve. As Jesus told his disciples, he is not going to leave us as orphans. He is going to send his Spirit to give us new powers.

Read the following six Reflections on what we can do to better prepare ourselves for the Spirit's work. These practices are organized around the acronym GROWTH:

> **G**o to God in Prayer and Worship
> **R**ead God's Word for You
> **O**bey the Challenge to Deny Yourself
> **W**itness through Servant Behavior
> **T**rust God in a New Venture
> **H**umble Yourself with a Discipline

Go to God in Prayer and Worship

Almost all (85%) Christians talk to God in their own words. This finding is from a major research project I did years ago on the prayer practices of ordinary Christians. What they do can be called conversational prayer. One respondent explained that while he does have time set aside for prayer, he enjoys spontaneity. "I try to talk with God when the thought or feeling strikes me. Some days I pray quite a bit, others not such much. I have some special times with God but usually prayer and contemplation come at random."

We tend to admire those who spend a long time in prayer. They must be especially devout. The rest of us without the gift of intercession usually feel guilty in comparison. Yet highly admired Christian leaders taught otherwise. Augustine of Hippo (5th century) preferred "very brief, quickly dispatched prayers." Thomas Aquinas (13th century) held that frequency, not length, is the important issue in prayer. Frequent short prayers are of more worth than a few lengthy prayers.

Martin Luther (16th century) recommended prayers to be numerous but short in duration. The fewer the words the better the prayer. Few words and much meaning is Christian. Many words and little meaning is pagan. Jacob Boehme (17th century) advised that "many words are not needed, but only a believing, repentant soul.

Dwight Moody (19th century) carried this view over to public prayer. "A man who prays much in private will make short prayers in public." He regarded lengthy public prayers as something akin to religious pretension.

Donald Bloesch (20th century) concluded that what characterized the great saints was not so much involvement in one single protracted or endless repetition of prayer formulas, but rather the practice of constantly waiting on the Lord, of praying inwardly even when outwardly occupied in daily tasks.

Going to God in Prayer and Worship is the most fundamental practice for being drawn closer to God in everyday living. Prayer is done alone or in small groups. Worship is done in larger assemblies. It is the same relationship of practicing your relationship with God.

What Prayer Accomplishes

The central questions are what these practices do *for you* and what they do *for others.*

For you, prayer turns your thoughts God-ward. "Draw near to God and he will draw near to you" (James 4:8). When those thoughts are shaped by biblical truths, they expose you to the Holy Spirit's work on your inner being. From such heart-work come the love, joy, peace and trust that deliver to you more of the abundant life Jesus came to bring.

What your prayers and worship don't do is earn you more credit in God's eyes. For centuries church life was approached as a duty we owe to God. The goal would be to build up a more virtuous, God-pleasing life that earns God's favor.

Rather than just *duty*, prayer and worship are *opportunities* to experience more of God's blessings in this life on the way to heaven. In Christ's redeeming work we already have the salvation that God promises for the next life. He also promises to send his Holy Spirit and the fruit he can produce for a better life now. We daily have opportunity to draw upon his potential for life-changing power. The Lord's Prayer is the ultimate expression of the prayer relationship. Recognize that this prayer is in the context of a lengthier teaching, which Jesus ends with the promise: "How much more will your Father in heaven give the Holy Spirit to those who ask him!" (Luke 11: 14). Prayer is asking for this special power that changes lives.

Church teachings with little appreciation of the Spirit's work inevitably approach our routine relationship with God as something we do. This approach too often becomes a guilt-inducing burden for many believers. Better it is to approach prayer as a refreshing opportunity.

Intercessory Prayer

Intercessory prayer is done *for others*. What it accomplishes is more difficult to answer. This is because of a teaching that God has already made up his mind what will happen in your life and that of others. Such is the message especially in John Calvin's doctrine of double predestination—some are predestined to salvation and others are predestined to damnation. God is sovereign and determines all human affairs. This understanding leaves little room for prayer requests for others. Yet even Calvin himself regularly participated in congregational prayers and petitions. Logic in relating to God has its limits.

A more biblical teaching is that God can indeed change his mind in response to prayers. Evidence is in Abraham's bargaining with God to spare those in Sodom, and God agreed. Two of Jesus' parables endorse persistence in prayer. One is the man who repeatedly knocks on his neighbor's door for bread for an unexpected guest. The other is the widow who nagged the judge with her petitions. In both cases, their persistence brought a favorable result. Won't such prayer make a difference when addressed not to a grouchy neighbor but to the loving Father?

How much difference do the number of words make in our prayers? Are they even necessary? Will many words bring a better result? Not really. Thinking that many words will persuade God is a form of works righteousness. What's important is the underlying attitude of dependence on God, who loves and responds like a parent.

Are words even necessary? No. Words are a means of expressing thoughts. It's the thoughts about God and others that count. Words without thought are empty. Humility and dependence are the key to exercising the basic relationship to God.

In my randomly sampled prayer research, about half reported a deep sense of peace and a strong presence of God in their prayers. One young woman reported that "I am often moved to tears during prayer, either with joy or fear, I guess." A young mother related that "Sometimes I am able to set aside time to play the piano and sing my prayers to God. I think I feel closest to God in prayer when it is through a song." A recovering alcoholic wrote, "If I stop just moments to pray and make amends, I can enjoy a 'peace of mind' that is mind boggling."

Improving Prayer Life

One of the surprises in the research was that four out of five (80%) felt they would like to improve their prayer life. That's valuable information for church leaders wanting to better connect with participants. Churches become more effective as they find spiritual needs and fill them. Give high priority to helping church participants grow in their personal prayer relationship with God. The response will be very good.

The biggest surprise in the research was that fully half of these ordinary believers declared that prayer is the most satisfying experience in their life!! That's an extreme statement. Who would have guessed?

How can you improve your prayer life? The starting point is finding the personal benefits of peace and power in your practice. Don't just do what somebody else finds satisfying. If you don't experience benefits, you probably won't do it long. Learn conversational prayer. Enjoy spontaneity. Find times and places that work for you, like talking with God on your drive to work. Try participating in a prayer group. What you are looking for is the feeling of the presence of God with the peace and power the Spirit can bring.

Those who regularly experience the benefits of prayer find themselves praying more often. Those who pray often are the ones who find prayer the most satisfying experience in their lives. Try it.

Read God's Word for You

"Nothing has a greater impact on spiritual growth than reflection on Scripture." Such is the conclusion of a massive study that gathered data from participants in 1,000 congregations of a cross-section of Protestant denominations.

Note the key word "reflection" on Scripture. God's Word comes in two forms. One is the familiar Bible of almost 800,000 words over about 1,000 pages. The other is the Word that was God expressing himself in creation and becoming flesh in Jesus. This Word is the creative force that changes lives today.

There are two ways to read the Bible. One is for *information*. The other is for *formation*. The amount of information is overwhelming, especially those covering the 1,500 years of the Old Testament. The New Testament is only one fifth the total length and is easier, covering only about 100 years. It also focuses better on grace-centered living.

While reading the Bible is basic, the key for spiritual growth is reflecting on what you read with the question, "What does this mean for me now?" This is reading for *formation*. Reading for *information* amounts to preparation for the formation payoff.

In reading Scripture for formation, the four Gospels are easier to apply to a person's life today because they tell us what Jesus did and the way he guided and challenged those around him. We can imagine ourselves in their place. Within the Gospels, Jesus' parables are the easiest to apply to my personal life now. One of the most popular is the proud Pharisee bragging about what he did for God and the humble Tax Collector who simply said, God have mercy on mercy on me, a sinner. Where have you been proud of what you are doing for God? How and where could you be more humble in your daily walk? That's *formation*.

Will You Be In-Spirited?

The 800,000-word Bible presents divinely inspired truth. Inspired means in-Spirited. The creative Spirit was at work among the various authors whose words we read. That creative Word became flesh and made his dwelling among us in the person of Jesus of Nazareth. Now ascended, he and the Father delegate that creative force to his Spirit, who dwells among us today.

Here's the issue. Will the readers of the 800,00 words be creatively "in-Spirited" also? They will if they are willing to move beyond reading for *information* to reading for *formation*. This amounts to being shaped by the Spirit.

Paul urged that his readers "be transformed by the renewing of your mind. Then you will be able to test and approve what God's will is" (Romans 12:2). We add, God's will for you. It is certainly true for all people. But when you are reading for formation, the emphasis is on what this creative Word means for you personally. How will your life be transformed by what you are hearing from God? Elsewhere, Paul described how "we are being transformed into Christ's likeness with ever-increasing glory, which comes from the Lord, who is the Spirit." (2 Cor 3: 18).

The Bible is not meant to be read cover to cover. Most readers get bogged down in Leviticus and Numbers and give up. It is a collection of God-inspired writings of different types of literature, including the poetry of the Psalms and the symbolism of Revelation, parts of which were not meant to be taken literally Each book needs to be interpreted according to the type of literature it is. Yet Scripture is infallible in what it teaches about the relation between God and his people.

How to Absorb God's Word

How do you read God's Word in order to be shaped by the Spirit? Slowly and with the realization that the Spirit comes at his initiative. What you can do is take the initiative to place yourself in the Spirit's workshop. Reading by yourself is a good start. To Scriptures themselves, add reading well-written devotionals that interpret a passage and apply it to daily living. But the best workshop is where the Word is being shared and applied by others around you. That happens especially in small groups that discuss the meaning of a particular Word for them personally.

Traditionally, most believers absorbed God's truth through listening to sermons. In earlier centuries most believers were illiterate. Still today in our developed society many cannot read well. It is a learned skill. Also, some are dyslexic. The usual advice to just "read the Word" has limited value to those for whom reading is a challenge.

Sermons are most productive when they move beyond conveying biblical information. The payoff is the application, which many preachers don't do well. As a preacher, I earlier thought my job was simply to announce and explain biblical truths. Over the years I grew more conscious of the need to also offer practical illustrations and applications, and I admire preachers who do that well. Preaching for formation is an advanced skill.

I have felt in-Spirited to think and write about the role of the Holy Spirit in personal and church life. This kind of inspiration is not at all on the level of the inspired writers of Scriptures. But I am convinced the Spirit has been at work in me and through my words in the lives and ministries of others. What a privilege!

Has Christ's Spirit inspired you to take some action or speak some words that had a spiritual impact on others? Almost certainly. We in traditional churches have had many experiences of the Spirit. But we have not been taught the meaning. Let the Spirit do more of his formative work in you. When you are not sure you are hearing the Spirit right, seek the perspective of mature Christians who know you. Pray for the courage to follow where the Spirit is leading.

Paul told the Corinthians that he gave them milk, not yet solid food. What is the solid food he had in mind? I used to think it was doctrinal information in ever greater detail. But now I see it is about how to live together in a fellowship of Christ. There is ever more to learn about relationships in church communities and how these can be more fruitful through formation by the Spirit.

Meditation

Practicing "mindfulness" has become a popular term, typically in the context of counseling. Psychologists are re-discovering the value of mindfulness in coping with the challenges of modern living. The current version traces its origins to Buddha. But we Christians have a longer heritage, going back to the psalmist whose delight is in the law of the Lord, on which Word he meditates day and night.

The modern practice of mindfulness teaches how to focus on a single word or phrase, called a mantra, for as long as possible. God's people have been focusing on certain Bible passages since the beginning. Their mantras can be seen on wall plaques in the home or heard in phrases in a conversation. Some are: I can do all things through him who *strengthens me*. In all things *God works for the good* of those who love him. Those who hope in the Lord will *soar on wings like eagles*. Such focus is basic to formation through the Word.

Theologically trained preachers tend to make the biblical Word complicated. The Bible has so much information. Most believers, in my experience, keep it simple in living out their daily relationship with God. Strengthen their core convictions with care, so they are slowly formed by the in-Spirited Word, not just exposed to biblical information that passes them by.

Obey the Challenge to Deny Yourself

Military history fascinates me. It presents real-life stories of leaders making decisions and facing the consequences in terms of reaching some objective. The *strategos,* in Greek, is the general who makes the big decisions about where to place troops and equipment and when to go into action. In the Korean War the Allied forces were on the defensive and rapidly losing ground. Rather than fight the enemy head on, Gen. Douglas MacArthur did the unexpected and landed troops on their flank at Inchon and forced a hasty retreat that changed the momentum of the war.

Businesses and organizations make strategic decisions about what they will emphasize and how they will use their resources. Churches, too, have to make such strategic choices in times of rapid social change.

Here the focus is on individual strategic choices in the Christian life. The major choice, of course, is what to do about gaining eternal life in heaven at the end of this life on earth. Protestants stress that the next life is a gift based on the redemption Jesus Christ won for us. It is by grace you are saved, not by works. This is counter-intuitive in a world where you get what you earn.

My emphasis, here, is on our daily walk with Jesus. What is your strategy for living the Christian life for all it is worth? Will you be timid and just live day by day, or will you reach out for more of what God offers? What do you expect of him?

Peter had a major conflict with Jesus about strategy. Jesus predicted his death. Peter rebuked him for giving up. He was expecting this new kind of rabbi to win a big victory. Jesus in turn rebuked Peter for not having in mind the things of God, but the things of men. Then Jesus laid out his strategy of finding the good life God offers. "If anyone would come after me, he must deny himself and take up his cross and follow me. Whoever wants to save his life will lose it, but whoever loses his life for me will find it" (Matthew 16: 24). Imagine Peter thinking, *That's it? That doesn't make any sense!*

Jesus' Strategy for Winning by Losing

Jesus' strategy for gaining the good life is to let the Holy Spirit teach you how to respond to his expectation that you love one another. You are not on your own. The desired outcome—victory, if you will—is that you love God and one another. You lose by continuing to depend on your own wits and abilities to work out your relationship with God. Give up dependence on yourself and you will find that you have gained an even more abundant life than you could on your own.

Jesus explained his strategy in a conversation with his disciples after the Passover meal he shared on Maundy Thursday. It is recorded at length in John 14-16. Trust the Father, he started out. He sent me, his Son, so that you may know him and discover how to love him and one another. He sent me to show you his expectations. He and I will give you the Holy Spirit, whom only my followers will understand and not others. I will not leave you as orphans. After I have gone away, this Spirit will teach you all things and remind you of everything I taught you. This way you will find peace unlike anything the world offers.

Pay Attention to God's Expectations

In Jesus' strategy session, he used the words "obey" and "command" eight times. They must be basic to his approach. It would be easy to think of God's plan in military terms. Having served as a chaplain in the Navy Reserves for many years, I have a sense of what that can mean in the military context of orders issued by a superior about behavior that is required, regardless of what you think about it. But such command-and-obey structure can't be the meaning in this context because blind obedience to a superior's commands is the way of the world, which is not what Jesus promoted. Again and again, he got angry with the Pharisees that demanded blind obedience to hundreds of religious laws.

There must be a softer interpretation of "obey my commands." We have a translation issue. "Expectation" is a fitting translation of command. Jesus was telling his disciples what is expected of them in this new plan that will be empowered by the Spirit he and the Father will send.

"Obey" in the original conveys the sense of maintaining or preserving. I think what Jesus is telling his followers is to pay attention to, stay focused on the expectation he sets forth. When Jesus said, "My expectation is this: Love one another as I have loved you," he did not have in mind a military command.

Accept the Challenge To Deny Yourself

"Challenge" is another way to translate a command. At another time, Jesus offered a different perspective on his strategy. A wealthy young man approached him and asked, What must I do to inherit eternal life? One of the basics of strategic planning is to clarify the objective. This man was not just asking about how to get to heaven at the end of life. He wanted to know how to get the good life, the life eternal.

Jesus said he should obey the commandments. Which ones? All of them. This I have done, replied the young man. Then Jesus surprised him. Now sell all your possessions and give to the poor. Then follow me. This answer flabbergasted the man. He was not ready for such a drastic step and went away sad.

Jesus had confronted him with a challenge, not a command. He does not expect his followers to have no wealth. What he does expect is that they not let themselves lose focus on greater things by focusing only on what this world offers. Be sure to use God's special blessings wisely for the benefit of others.

The name of this third practice is Obey the Challenge to Deny Yourself. I would have preferred Accept the Challenge. But my challenge at hand is to work with the acronym GROWTH. So "Obey" it is, with the understandings I have laid out.

The Holy Spirit's Role in Jesus's Strategy

Towards the beginning of the strategy session with his disciples, Jesus explained the means by which his people will be able to put his expectations into action. A good strategy always includes provision for the necessary resources. Jesus explains how he is asking his Father to give disciples a second helper besides Jesus himself. He will leave them, but this Strengthener will stay with them forever. This Advocate, the Spirit of truth, will teach them everything they will need to know. Teaching is not just head knowledge. He will influence and enable them to continue Jesus' ministry.

Without his Spirit as Enabler, Jesus' strategic plan won't work.

REFLECTION 18

Witness Through Servant Behavior

Are you an evangelist? Probably not. We hear stories of someone on an airplane talking with a seat mate and leading them to Christ. Most of us feel guilty when we are challenged to do such ministry. It is one of those "shoulds" that are often laid on us but really don't change our behavior. By one estimate, much less than 10% of church goers are natural evangelists.

But look at giving witness of your faith to others as a basic step in growing closer to God. It can push you out of your comfort zone and increase your dependence on God. It stretches you, like doing regular exercise to keep your body healthy. Give witness to others in order to stay fit in your spiritual health and even to grow in your faith.

Peter and John were ordinary men—illiterate, we are told. True, they had been with Jesus for three years, absorbing his fresh teaching, just like many ordinary Christians have been in church for years, absorbing biblical teachings. Witnessing in the temple, they were put on the spot. "By what power are you teaching in the temple?," the authorities demanded. Peter gave his testimony. Luke starts this story with the phrase that Peter was "filled with the Holy Spirit." Luke uses that phrase in at least eight different settings in his Gospel and the book of Acts. Someone was filled with the Spirit and did something with special conviction or wisdom.

You Will Be Filled With the Holy Spirit

What "filled with the Holy Spirit" means is very controversial in our times. Pentecostals use it to describe a special outpouring of the Spirit that enables a believer to speak in strange tongues. In fact, in many Pentecostal congregations you can't become a member without demonstrating what is called this second baptism of the Spirit. Most of the growth of Christianity in our times is in Pentecostal forms. If you are going to become a follower of Jesus, why not seek such peak special emotional experiences? The opportunity to "feel" the Spirit is attractive.

Most traditional Protestants can't go there. We value the priority of reason over emotions and rightly resist "irrational" expressions of God's presence in a person's life. But we can appreciate that the Holy Spirit will empower us when the time comes to give a witness to our faith. We can be filled with the Spirit in a special way when an occasion puts us on the spot to explain who we are and what we believe. We can trust God to send his Spirit to give us special bravery or wisdom when the occasion presents opportunity. After all, this is his promise.

Two Versions of Motivation for Witnessing

In their Gospels, Matthew and Luke give us two different versions of why and how to give witness. Matthew's is the familiar "Go and make disciples of all nations." Jesus started that commission with the declaration that he has all authority in heaven and on earth. This Great Commission comes across as a military command. You have your orders. You must obey. Now go do it. The problem is that this version does not work well today. In my experience it doesn't motivate much new behavior.

The motivation is better addressed in Luke's version. He simply predicts that you will be my witnesses. God is going to give you power from on high to do that. The Holy Spirit is going to empower you in ways that will surprise you. My Spirit, Jesus promises, will enable you will to be my witnesses to the end of the earth.

Witness is the fourth practice of the GROWTH scheme for positioning yourself to grow closer to God. Grow by responding to opportunities to explain who you are and what you believe. Witness to the Gospel wherever possible, whether in word or deed.

Confronting An Avalanche of Words

But how do you make your witness when we are all buried under an avalanche of words every day. We have all learned to fend off the advertisements we daily encounter by the dozens and hundreds. Ads themselves are now getting simplified to a quick succession of graphic images because words mean so little.

We in mainline churches are at an even greater disadvantage because we have a specialized church vocabulary developed over the centuries. For us, key biblical phrases can pack a powerful punch, like redemption, salvation, Jesus the Christ. But biblical literacy is fast receding in our current culture. Basic Bible stories draw a blank stare from so many young adults.

How do we break through the maze of words that surround everyone? It is hardly going to be by adding more words—at least not at the outset. The best witness today is the quality of life we Christians live day by day. Actions do speak louder than words. That's how the earliest Christians had their biggest impact. Observers were struck by how they loved each other.

What we can do today is let our acts of service and kindness make an impact that draws attention to our church of believers who are intent on serving our community and demonstrating that our church is a "loving" place. Call that Servant Evangelism.

Servant Evangelism

Servant Evangelism is a term that reached prominence through the ministry of Steve Sjogren when he was pastor of the Vineyard Community Church in Columbus, Ohio. His classic example was showing up at a local business with mop and bucket in hand and asking permission to clean their toilets—something that is clearly servant behavior. It becomes a witness when leaving a calling card to identify the congregation on behalf of which this act was done. Other examples are to give away free coffee to those standing in line somewhere, or to do free gift-wrapping at Christmas, or to give away popsicles on a hot day.

Our church twice a year does a Servant Saturday event. It is surprisingly popular, with about three hundred showing up. Many make it a family affair. We work with the city to identify those in need, typically elderly residents who can't keep up with cleaning and yard work. I remember pulling weeds in a Catholic widow's yard and asking myself why I was doing so when I had lots of weeds in my own yard. The answer came, That's what Christians do; we serve others. These events are faith affirming experiences for me personally. They become a faith witness when we identify ourselves as member of our congregation.

Part of the challenge traditional churches face today is to be known for doing what churches are supposed to do—be centers for offering spiritual growth in Christ and for ministering to those in need. Look for ways to do that through Servant Behavior.

Trust God in a New Venture

My focus is on Six Practices for Spiritual Growth. My intent is to make the basics of such formation by the Spirit as practical as possible.

The fifth practice is learning to trust God. Everyday life teaches lessons of trust for believers as we learn to accept what appear to be bad things happening in our lives, relationships, illnesses and finances. We learn new levels of letting go and trusting God. Accepting downturns can be called *passive* faith.

Active faith is learning to trust God in a new venture. It's the kind of trust Abraham in the Genesis story had when he heard God's call to take his son Isaac up into a mountain to make a sacrifice, only to find out the sacrifice was going to be his son. Killing him made absolutely no sense, especially given God's earlier promise that through this son Abraham would become the father of the great nation of God's people. Yet, knife in hand, he was ready to do the deed. He thereby passed the test. Instead, God provided a sacrificial lamb. Over the centuries Abraham's faith has been recognized as the greatest among God's people.

Nineteenth-century Danish philosopher Soren Kierkegaard made Abraham's test the basis of his most popular book *Fear and Trembling*. There he gave us the memorable phrase "the leap of faith." Learn to grow in your relationship with Christ by purposefully taking leaps of faith beyond what you would ordinarily do.

Seven Realities of Experiencing God

In recent decades millions of Christians have learned how to know and do God's will through Henry Blackaby's workbook *Experiencing God*, which is very popular in Baptist circles. He describes seven realities involved in experiencing God: 1) Recognize that God is at work in your life and that 2) he pursues a love relationship with you. 3) He invites you to join him and 4) he speaks to you. Key is 5) a crisis of faith when you realize you cannot do on your own what God is asking, and you realize that 6) if God doesn't help you will fail. Growth continues through 7) ultimate surrender to God so his will, not yours, be done.

That fourth reality assumes that I as a believer have a relationship with God in which I hear him calling me to do something. Accepting that God speaks to us today as he did to people in biblical times is a big step for many traditional Christians.

Most formative is the fifth reality of realizing that on your own you cannot do what God is asking. It is natural to want a sure thing before we invest time and energy. But being timid does not produce growth. As the writer of Hebrews tells us, faith is being sure of what we hope for and certain of what we do not see. Remember, while faith is a noun it is also a verb meaning to trust. The growth challenge is to trust outcomes that are not visibly certain.

Paul sets this process of growth in the context of the Holy Spirit working within us. The Spirit is the one who calls. The Spirit builds our confidence. He enables us to surrender to God's will. What if this new venture fails? The Spirit is there to help us process what happened. He will build us up so we are ready to try again with a new venture. For growth, the constant challenge is to put your trust to the test.

"The Holy Spirit is always a mystery," as J. Harold Ellens tells us, "an intriguing agent of God, full of intimations of God's nature, truth, and grace. These intimations speak spontaneously to our natures as we hunger for God. One must have the eyes to see and the ears to hear, of course. It is an intriguing and exciting thing indeed to live life always consciously anticipating how the Holy Spirit of God will show up around the next corner. The Spirit always does if we are expecting him."

My Challenging New Ventures

Blackaby's basic illustration is planting a new church. That challenge was a significant component of my personal spiritual growth. I had heard of a church planting opportunity in my hometown of Cleveland. I was teaching a two-week course of church management to pastors, and several came back from the weekend excited about a church plant they had visited. Then and there I knew what I was called to do. Many were the times I thought I was facing failure. But God provided opportunities. Under a successor, a healthy mid-size congregation with its own building is the result.

Over the years I have tried different forms of ministry and outreach. Many did not "work" in terms of attracting enough participants to continue. If pastors have not failed in a ministry, they are probably not trying hard enough. Untested, many are probably also not growing much in their personal spirituality.

Pray, Meditate and Be Tested

Being tested was one of the three basics of spiritual formation Martin Luther featured in the Latin phrase *oratio, meditatio, tentatio*—pray, meditate and be tested. This is the path he laid out especially for those wanting to become ministers.

Paul laid out a similar sequence, which I offer here with my own translation. Stress produces persistence, which produces discovery (character), which produces trust (Romans 5: 3,4). The stress of suffering a negative affliction in our lives is learning passive trust. The stress of Trusting God in a New Venture presents opportunities for active trust. Deliberately facing such self-imposed stress can be productive. Actively choosing to place yourself in a stressful challenge produces a track record of persistence that offers discovery that develops proof of character. What are you proving? That God can be trusted to see you through to new accomplishments, especially those in service to the Gospel.

Out of this process of learning trust comes new hope. "Hope does not disappoint us, because God has poured out his love into our hearts by the Holy Spirit, whom he has given us" (Romans 5:5). For believers, Christ's Spirit is the engine that drives this progression. What you are testing is the Spirit's guidance and power. For Paul, hope is in a triad along with the faith and the love he features. All three are gifts generated by the Spirit in believers. Do you want to grow into more faith, hope and love? Try to Trust God in a New Venture.

Planting a new church is a tall challenge. Traditional mainline denominations have a very poor track record in recent decades. Yet there is hope. The church I serve made four attempts to plant new congregations. Three succeeded. New Protestant churches keep popping up in many communities. Observing such successes can offer opportunity to test out some new forms of outreach and ministry.

A church life that is healthy will offer opportunities to reach out and bear fruit in the lives of others. Such churches will also offer encouragement and advice. They can help individuals assess fitness for a new ministry of serving others. Where there is failure, they can provide perspective and highlight lessons learned in growing closer to God.

A healthy congregation teaches how to Trust God in a New Venture. A healthy Christian learns to do the same!

Humble Yourself with a Discipline

During the Pandemic I would drive by a house with a yard sign announcing, "I Am A Health Care Hero." What an odd thing to boast about. Real heroes don't brag. Certainly, front-line health care providers were heroes. But it's like combat veterans whose bravery was recognized by a medal, like the Silver Star or Medal of Honor. Many such awardees discuss how uncomfortable they are for being singled out among others who fought in the same situation. Most put their medals away rather than brag on them.

So it is with humility. Humble people don't go around bragging about how humble they are. That's a fundamental contradiction. True humility is not an accomplishment. It's an attitude that comes from within. What you can do is work on keeping yourself humble. You can choose disciplines for that purpose.

When I think of spiritual disciplines, I recall visiting the afternoon service (*None*) of a large Trappist monastery in Rome. The setting was beautiful, with an ornate sanctuary and the procession of monks two by two in their special habits, who then solemnly chanted the Psalms. But I also recall thinking I could never do this; it must be really boring doing the same thing fives time a day every day. It seemed so grim.

But there are other spiritual disciplines everyday Christian can commit themselves to. Richard Foster is the most popular recent writer on spiritual disciplines for Protestants. His book is *Celebration of Discipline: The Path to Spiritual Growth*. He recognizes three categories: Inward, Outward and Corporate Disciplines.

Three Kinds of Disciplines

The Inward Disciplines are meditation, prayer, fasting and study. Prayer is basic for most practicing Christians. Try different approaches to strengthening your prayer life until you find what works best for you. Meditation amounts to reading God's Word for formation. Fasting never caught on among Protestants. Study is my chosen discipline. I love probing Scriptures to understand what is special about spiritual and church life in view of behavioral insights.

The Outward Disciplines are simplicity, solitude, submission and service. Service to others is a major emphasis among Protestants. Submission is so significant that I recognize it in the third of the seven basic practices: Obey the Challenge to Deny Yourself. It has been particularly productive in my personal spiritual life.

The Corporate Disciplines are confession, worship, guidance and celebration. While historically Protestants have not looked favorably on individual spiritual disciplines, we do practice weekly worship. Most congregations have occasional celebrations, typically around some sort of shared meal. Guidance for most is a new frontier. This is more than pastoral counseling about specific problems or situations. It can be a monthly session exploring steps an individual Christian can take to grow into a closer relationship with God. I have served as a spiritual director. I think the counselees made progress in their personal journey. I do know I found those sessions spiritually productive for me personally.

Confession of Sins

Ordinarily, God can't do much with you when you are full of yourself. That's why a discipline of emptying yourself is so important for spiritual growth. This is done through regular repentance of sins. Martin Luther urged a daily repentance of drowning out the old nature and letting the new nature in Christ come forth.

Here are some suggestions for improving the weekly repentance in the worship services of many traditional churches. The hymnal uses the same set of words every week. Frequently these are recited by rote without much thought. I have difficulties with pastors who write up their own confession for everyone to say together. So often they put words in my mouth about specific sins I can't identify with. I find myself getting peevish and lose my focus on God.

What I do find more helpful is the worship leader informally guiding me through my recent relationships with God and those around me. What do I wish I had done better in the last week or two? When did I not keep God first in my thinking and dealing with others? I resist being led to confess something about conditions over which I have no control. The purpose for this confession is to straighten out my personal relationship with God. It is not the occasion to campaign for social justice.

Dallas Willard offers a helpful perspective on the disciplines, contrasting spiritual church life with individual spirituality. "A spiritual life consists in that range of activities in which people cooperatively interact with God. Spirituality deals with another reality. It is absolutely indispensable to keep before us the fact that it is more than a "commitment" or a "life-style," even though a commitment and life-style will come from it. The disciplines show us how we can "offer our bodies as living sacrifices, holy and acceptable unto God."

Pride

The opposite of humility is pride. It's a natural human instinct to want to take pride in what we have accomplished. The need to be admired for what we have done is the fourth category in the classic motivational hierarchy of needs. We want to increase our personal status above those around us. But pride in the Christian life can be a trap that ensnares those who want to grow closer to God. It can easily lead to taking our eyes off God's blessings in order to highlight what we have done. I personally struggle with pride because indeed I have accomplished a lot. The corrective for me is to recall the unusual providential acts of God that have presented special opportunities. A stress-related clinical depression helped to break me from dependence on myself. I consciously have to humble myself when that urge to boast presents itself.

Pride is an occupational hazard in ministry. Particularly irksome are pastors who let it be known how they grew a church from a lower number to a higher one in attendance. I want to challenge them with Paul's explanation that he planted the seed, Apollos watered it, but God made it grow. Especially troublesome are pastors who seem to base their ministry identity on a special set of doctrines to which they give their allegiance. Biblical doctrine is basic. Also basic is an initial attitude of serving God creatively and energetically—and humbly—where he has placed us.

G-R-O-W-T-H

Are you serious about wanting to become more like Christ in your daily living? That's hard to do on our own strength. Jesus' strategy depends on empowerment by his Spirit that he sends to continue his work. Our role is to place ourselves where he can most readily change our motivation.

> **Go to God in Prayer and Worship**
> **Hear God's Word for You**
> **Obey the Challenge to Deny Yourself**
> **Witness through Servant Behavior**
> **Trust God in a New Venture**
> **Humble Yourself with a Discipline**

Calling To a Culture Or To a Relationship with Christ?

Martin Luther divided the work of the Holy Spirit into the four functions of calling, gathering, enlightening and sanctifying followers of Christ. These next reflections address ministries of calling.

Calling to follow Christ seemed so simple at first. John the Baptist pointed to Jesus as the expected Lamb of God. Two of John's disciples turned to Jesus, who asked what they wanted. To see where you are staying, they replied, curious about what differences he makes in life. Jesus challenged them to come and see. Andrew, Peter, then Phillip and Nathanael responded. Thus began the momentum for calling others to follow Christ.

After Pentecost the momentum of call and response brought moderate growth for the first three hundred years of the spread of Christianity. Then Emperor Constantine recognized Christianity as the preferred religion of the Roman Empire, and growth was explosive. Now there were social advantages to being a Christian. Calling became easier. For most of Christian church history there remained social advantages to being a follower of Christ. Such were the pressures in the Reformation churches. The ministry of calling stayed simple. Christianity was something you were born into. Almost all lived in villages and small towns, so there were social pressures to conform. Among Christian immigrants to America, the ministry of calling remained simplified. Previous immigrants met the new ones and gathered them into church communities that shared the same language. The social pressures to conform were strong.

Calling into a Culture

In my home neighborhood in Cleveland, the story is told of how in the 1870s the pastor from the new Immanuel Lutheran Church and the priest of the new St. Michael Catholic Church would join together and knock on doors along newly developed streets, one on each side. They asked whether each family was Lutheran or Catholic. At the end of the street, they swapped names. The challenge then was for each to gather those families into the appropriate flock. Calling ministries could not get much simpler.

What made the process so easy is that these mostly German immigrants self-identified with their home culture, which typically was either Catholic or Lutheran. The attraction was to rebuild the community they left behind. For many, central to that old community was church. But the church they and their leaders had in mind was mostly the culture of values and behaviors they associated with church. A culture is the set of beliefs, values and behaviors a community passes on to a new generation. In traditional German church culture, the beliefs were left to the pastor to define and explain. Members were taught the Catechism, which mostly passes on head knowledge without much provision for heart conviction.

Called Into a Personal Relationship with Christ

Church bodies that had their roots in European cultures never had to develop strong ministries of calling others to follow Christ. We could rely on cultural pressures, which are now disappearing among young adults who are several generations removed from their great-grandparents' immigrant roots. We traditional churches now face the more difficult task of calling people not into a church culture but into a personal relationship with Christ.

There are several problems with church lived out as a social culture. Basic is that this does not square well with the New Testament understanding of church called together by the work of the Holy Spirit. The second, more practical difficulty is what happens when that culture does not transfer to succeeding generations. Then you are left with congregations of mostly older members that have diminished ability to attract and hold young families.

The issue is, which is more basic to being a Christ follower? Is it the distinct traditions of values and behaviors of a church culture? Or are the personal convictions of those called together to be church more fundamental? Reaching out to those already in the tradition is easier. The job is much more demanding to call people into a relationship with Christ. That's Holy Spirit work. Thus our human effort is done better when we recognize the Spirit's ways and let his movement shape our ministries.

The Perils of Cultural Superiority

Lutheran church culture presents a special problem for ministering within the American culture. We come with an air of superiority. That's a common trait among Germans. It shows itself in an unwillingness to learn from the ministries of other churches or in a smug tendency to run down any ministries that other churches are doing. We do so to our loss.

My consistent message over several decades is to visit churches that shows evidence of effective ministry today. Check them out. See what you can learn. Some pastors have done so. Most have resisted. For them, if something does not carry the label Lutheran, it does not merit discussion.

Formative for me was the seven years I spent as vice president and faculty member at Fuller Seminary, often considered the flagship of Evangelical seminaries. I learned a lot and absorbed a taste for pastoral ministry I had not had before. One learning is that conservative Evangelicals find it hard to work with conservative Lutherans, who in their Germanic way want to take over and control whatever the project is. During those years, mission-minded Lutherans expressed interest in what I was learning in that community, which I addressed in the book *Evangelical Style and Lutheran Substance*. But church officials marginalized what they regarded as insufficiently and indistinctively Lutheran.

Where is the Holy Spirit in Our Ministries of Calling?

Where was the Holy Spirit in these simplified calling ministries of traditionalists? We confess that he was somewhere and somehow in the background, but we had little need to pin down just where and how. Other branches in the American Protestantism did develop maps. Revivalists featured human decision as the key component and expected the Spirit to move through the pressure of an altar call to bring the desired results. Pentecostals featured human emotions and relied on highly emotional experiences through which the Spirit was supposed to work. But neither approach does justice to the key Reformation emphasis on God's grace rather than human effort as the basis for our relationship with God.

The Apostle Paul remains the key guide. As central as grace is to his theology, the Holy Spirit is even more central. At least by the numbers, he referred to the Spirit twice as often as he did to grace. For him, the Holy Spirit was basic to any ministry he was doing. This Spirit influences human spirit and changes hearts. Look for him where motivations are changing.

Spirit-inspired church life is different from what happens in social organizations. For several decades after World War II the Red Cross and fraternal associations were taken as a model for many Protestant churches trying to improve their ministries. But the results were disappointing because those methods depend on just human energy. The challenge for mainline traditional congregations is to learn how to unleash Spirit energy.

Martin Luther was an avid disciple of Paul. Traditional churches in the Reformation heritage can rediscover mission strengths by developing Pauline ministries that are both grace focused and Spirit shaped.

Overcoming Church Cultural Barriers Today

The book *Mission at Nuremberg* by Tim Townsend tells the story of U.S. Army Chaplain Henry Gericke, who was assigned to minister to the Nazi war criminals at the 1945 Nuremberg trials. He became respected and effective, at least as measured by bringing several to repentance. He served his charges in many practical ways, including looking after their families. Gericke offered a simple explanation for his efforts on behalf of those he wanted to call back to faith. They have to like you before they will listen to you. Theodore Roosevelt said much the same thing. "People don't care how much you know until they know how much you care."

What a simple mission strategy for presenting the Gospel. Meet those you want reach where they are. Respect them. Fill what needs of theirs you can. Help them understand God's grace as you have experienced it. Participate in the Spirit's work by reducing as many social barriers as possible.

The Biblical Strategy for Calling Others To Christ

Paul developed that basic strategy by explaining, "I have become all things to all men so that by all possible means I might save some. I do this for the sake of the Gospel" (1 Corinthians 9: 22). The new community of Christ-followers started out within the Jewish culture of laws and rituals. Paul's specialty was reaching out to "others" (Gentiles) by emphasizing what God does for them in his grace, not what they need to do for him. Although he had freedom in Christ, he made himself as a slave to others to meet them where they are.

We believe it is the Holy Spirit who does the work of softening individual hearts to turn them to Christ. What we can learn from Paul is the importance of reducing barriers the Spirit has to work against to have personal breakthroughs. Call those cultural barriers. Paul faced two different cultures: the well-developed Jewish culture as well as also the more dominant culture of the customs and rituals for revering the pagan gods. He advised, Don't get trapped in either one. Focus on calling unbelievers into a living relationship with the biblical God. At the Apostolic Convention that gave Paul his commission for mission to Gentiles (Acts 15), Peter pronounced the verdict that we should not make it hard for those who are turning to God. Consistent with apostolic teaching, keep the cultural barriers as low as possible to welcome into a fellowship of Christ those who are convicted to be followers of Christ's way.

Confronting Church Culture Barriers Today

I grew up in a vibrant city-wide ethnic German church community of tens of thousands. Church life was exciting, with big rallies that drew thousands and enough grade schools to have sports leagues. My congregation was one of four churches of our brand in half a square mile. Then the neighborhood changed. Year by year the ethnic Germans moved out to the suburbs, and attendance declined until the church closed in 1976. My pastor father diligently worked the neighborhood and had a breakthrough with a large family from West Virginia. But there was a cultural clash at church that stymied growth. Then came the Puerto Ricans and a new language barrier. The members from the old culture simply gave up in that location.

I carry with me a healthy respect for vibrant church cultures but also awareness of the barriers they can present—a perspective not shared by many traditionalists who have not ventured beyond their home culture. By personality, I am result oriented. I can't help but assess a church organization by the results of its ministries. The results for our brand have not been good in the last forty years. There is nothing in sight that would turn around this accelerating decline—unless change happens. Change is not going to happen without first being critical of our shortcomings today. I am proud of the Lutheran theology that I inherited and know very well. But I also recognize its blind spots.

Consider these three ways for my kind of traditionalists to improve our ministries of calling others to Christ.

Reduce Our Cultural Dysfunctions

I once did a workshop with pastors where I promoted shared prayer, with the suggestion they gather prayer groups at church in the evenings. One pastor objected that this would have the same people at church every evening. My response was that there is something wrong when organizational meetings take precedence over spiritual meetings. Such is the inclination among mainline churches.

In the 20th century, Lutheran worship services in most congregations got much more scripted and formal. Meanwhile, many congregations on their own initiative ventured into more informal contemporary worship that, well done, can draw more worshipers than the traditional service. Yet church officialdom takes no recognition of an obvious movement and provides no help for congregations to get better at doing it. That's a serious dysfunction church wide.

Traditional mainline churches historically present a sharp distinction between clergy, who do the ministry, and laity, who support them. Paul stressed that everyone is a minister. The mainline heritage has had a blind spot to better and more biblical ways of getting ministry done by many rather than just a few.

Greater Emphasis on Spiritual Experiences

For historical reasons the sequence of traditional mainline church life has been to start with children belonging to church through infant baptism, then having them profess their faith at confirmation and maybe hope for a personal spiritual experience later. That's not working well anymore.

Churches doing well today usually emphasize the opposite sequence. First aim for a personal, spiritual experiences. Then teach new believers the biblical faith they want to confess. Perhaps then they will be drawn into more active church life. There is no need, however, to choose one pattern over the other. Both can work. But emphasizing personal spiritual experiences seems to be working better in today's social culture.

Make Way for The Spirit

Mainline traditional heritage is to see ministry as a human effort. We profess but don't pay much attention to how ministry is really the work of the Spirit. Luther taught that it is the Spirit who calls, gathers, enlightens and sanctifies God's people. We can do a better job of developing our church ministries in ways that reduce barriers to how he works on people's hearts.

Head-First, Heart-First and the Bell-Shaped Curve

Much of what has happened to Protestant churches in America can be illustrated by the well-known bell-shaped normal distribution curve.

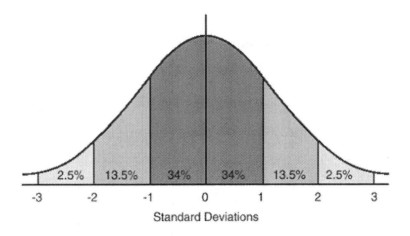

The top of the curve represents the mid-point in the distribution of certain characteristics over a large population. People who have more of that characteristic are on the right side. People with less are on the left side. The bottom of each side flattens out, and people on the far right and left are called outliers.

Take athleticism, for an example. Two thirds of a random sampling are roughly average, represented by the darker shade in the middle. The outliers on the right are high in athleticism (coordination, reflexes, speed). Although I lettered in high school, I discovered that I am really on the lower end of average. Good athletes playing tennis, racquetball or volleyball get frustrated with me because I don't return volleys very well. Feeling unwelcome, I haven't played sports for years.

Now consider people on a continuum from feeling to thinking about events around them. Some respond primarily according to their feelings. Others prefer to think through their response. Put the feelers on the left curve and call their response heart-first. Put the thinkers on the right curve and call their response head-first. "Average" people are a blend of heart and head.

When planning an event like worship, the thinkers are likely to dominate because they can offer persuasive reasons for their preferences. Most in the middle will go along. What will those further on the left do? They are likely to feel unwelcome and stop participating.

Head-First or Heart-First Churches

Traditional mainline denominations—like Presbyterian, Reformed, Methodist, Episcopal and Lutheran—have been decidedly head oriented. Founder Martin Luther was a university professor, and Reformed founder John Calvin was a very intelligent lawyer. Both were outliers on the right extreme. Those church bodies have since their beginning expected a university education from their pastors. Sermons are "heady," presenting theological reasoning based on the Bible.

The story of Christianity in America is full of break-off groups of believers who found themselves attracted to churches that appealed more to hearts than heads. The Great Revivals in previous centuries were based on emotional appeals to repent or to be overcome by the Holy Spirit in passionate calls to be changed.

The mainline denominations remained dominant up to World War II but peaked shortly afterwards and have been in decline since. Lots of analysis has gone into understanding why. One explanation is found in the bell-shaped distribution curve. The historic churches were shaped to appeal especially to the right side of the curve for head-first people. Those on the left curve of heart-first simply drifted away, feeling unwelcome.

In the realm of devotions, some people are comfortable expressing their emotions with high intensity. Others are emotionally more reserved. Traditional Protestant churches have their roots in Northern Europe among people who by instinct and culture are reserved about exhibiting emotions. In America, many from highly emotional cultures found other church expressions where they felt more welcome to feed their heart-first relationship with God.

What Would Jesus Do?

How would Jesus respond to the bell-shaped curve of people reacting feeling-first or thinking-first?

First of all, I think he would scold the mainline churches for being so narrow in their appeal. He would ask, What are you doing about the left side, those who are more emotionally heart-first?

Jesus himself was personally attracted to the left side of the curve. He respected them and in turn was respected by the ordinary people of his day, most of whom were illiterate. Repeatedly, he tangled in public with the scribes and Pharisees, who were the head-oriented scholars of that day. He used simple language and lots of illustrations and story parables. He drew the many to himself, not just a few.

What Should Traditional Churches Do Today?

To me, it seems obvious that the once-dominant mainline churches need to shift their focus more toward the center of the curve, to be more accommodating to those who react with feelings more than with reason. This would mean overcoming reservations about appealing to emotional experiences while still respecting the sensibilities of their traditional participants.

How can churches on the right curve do that? My advice is to look to the many community churches who are growing. Key for them is to show respect for all those who come to try them out. The ones I have observed are unapologetically committed to biblical truth as a much-appreciated source of authority for how to live. They emphasize good communication and emotion-touching, easily accessible singing. They are informal and personable.

Niche Churches

The alternative to moving more toward the center is to settle into a niche appealing only to a narrow segment of the whole distribution. Many of the mainline churches have become comfortable in the niche of being highly rational while de-emphasizing the supernatural ways of the supernatural God. In my own circles, many want the niche of highly formal liturgical ways of worshipping and doing ministry.

I don't want to be part of a niche church. God calls us to go out to all people. The way to get beyond head-first is to rediscover the Holy Spirit who was so basic to Paul's ministry. He specializes in touching hearts. We can see Christ's Spirit as a gentleman who will not coerce unwelcome behavior. He will, though, change motivations and lead us into becoming more joyfully like Christ. Having such an abundant life is appealing to both the right and the left side of the curve

Fields Ripe For Harvest

In Strange Rites: New Religions for a Godless World (2020) Tara Isabella Burton offers a dizzying description of movements that are changing the religious landscape. She posits a fundamental distinction between religion in general and institutional churches that come in many brands. While it is apparent a whole generation is bypassing institutional church life, most are not rejecting religion.

Rather, they are re-mixing the ingredients for their personal faith. "Today's Remixed reject authority, institution, creed and moral universalism. They value intuition, personal feelings and experiences. They want to rewrite their own scripts about how the universe and human beings operate. The Remixed don't want to receive doctrine, to assent automatically to a creed. They want to choose the personal path that feels more authentic, more meaningful, to them. They prioritize *intuitional* spirituality over *institutional* religion."

Some numbers will clarify the challenge. In 2007 15 percent of Americans called themselves religiously unaffiliated, meaning they did not consider themselves to be members of any traditional organized religion. By 2012 that number had risen to 20 percent. For adults under 30 that number is now about 40 percent. These can be described as the "Nones" that have no traditional religion. These are not atheists, who remain at about 7 percent of the population.

Burton observes: "We do not live in a godless world. Rather, we live in a profoundly anti-institutional one, where the proliferation of Internet creative culture and consumer capitalism has rendered us all simultaneously parishioner, high priest, and deity. America is not secular but simply spiritually self-focused. Anti-institutional, intuitional self-divinization is, at heart, the natural spirituality of Internet and smartphone culture."

What Caused the Shift?

Burton believes much of the responsibility for that shift belongs to institutions themselves. Traditional religions have not been able to offer compellingly meaningful accounts of the world, provide their members with purpose, foster sustainable communities, or put forth evocative rituals.

Perhaps most damaging to Evangelical institutional churches is their harsh denunciation of same sex relations, which are now taken by newer generations as a common-sense civil right above controversy. This hardened position has become a disconnect for so many. The solution is not to back off from the biblical position on same sex relationships, as many in mainline churches have done. The challenge is to express that morality with wisdom in the context of a loving community that maintains its integrity.

In Pagans and Christians in the City (2018) Steven D. Smith offers a provocative distinction between two kinds of religious belief. One he calls the paganism that locates the sacred *within* the world. The other, as practiced by Judaism and Christianity, places the sacred *outside* this world. The new intuitional spiritualities and movements are essentially pagan. That word is too negatively loaded to use it as a conversation starter. It does, though, point out a direction for developing conversations with the Remixed.

Paul's Approach

Paul knew real pagans. He met them on their own turf of Mars Hill in Athens, where he started his conversation by noting that among their many gods they had an altar to the unknown god. "Now what you worship as something unknown I am going to proclaim to you" (Romans 17: 23). He did so by declaring that the God he worships is not far from them. This God wants a relationship with them. He will no longer overlook ignorance but will come in judgment. This God has real power, which he proved by raising Jesus Christ from the dead. We read that some responded with a sneer, but others said, We want to hear you more on this subject.

The goal for Christian witness today is to conduct ourselves in ways that others say, I want to learn more about your God. What would Paul say if he faced our mixed-up spiritualities of today? He would not start out by condemning those he addressed. He would not just unload the Gospel in a nutshell. He would go to those he wanted to reach on their turf. He would recognize their problems and respect their issues. Then he would show how the biblical God has better answers for how to live. He would highlight the advantages of living true to God's way.

Paul's Four Steps

In his book *Plugged In* Daniel Strange analyzes Paul's approach. He did not come as bringing "religion" to them. He came addressing questions they were already asking, encouraging discussion of religious commitments they already have, and offering a way to mend their relationship with the God they were already seeking. Strange highlights four steps Paul took that we can take to reach out to the pagans of our day. The first is *Entering* by stepping into their world and listening to their story. Then *Exploring* by searching for elements of awe and grace in their lives. Step further into *Exposing* by showing up the idols as destructive frauds. Then comes *Evangelizing* by showing off the Gospel of Jesus Christ as subversive fulfillment.

Strange stresses that those we are engaging are real people. "That means communicating holistically and humanely. It demands love for, patience with and a "bearing with" tolerance of the other, which in the current climate is so counter-cultural. It requires the skills of listening carefully and slowly building trust. We need emotional intelligence to recognize how we listen and how we are heard."

Making Faith Magnetic

In his later book *Making Faith Magnetic,* Daniel Strange further offers the image of a magnet that attracts objects to it. Jesus is a magnet attracting all people to him. We are called to be magnets. Humans have a built-in "itch" that needs to be scratched in one way or another.

Drawing on the work of missiologist J. H. Bavinck, Strange offers five magnetic points. First, all those created by God have a built-in need to find a way to connect with others. Call that *Totality*. They are looking for a way to live, or *Norms*. They have an itch for a way out of their present situation, or *Deliverance*. They search for their destiny as a way to *Control* their lives. Fifth, they want a *Higher Power* as a way beyond where they are now.

Sixteen centuries ago, Bishop Augustine of Hippo confessed his personal itches in this famous phrase: You have made us for yourself, O Lord, and our hearts are restless until they rest in thee. As Tara Isabella Burton described the Remixed in *Strange Rites*, there is a whole lot of spiritual restlessness going on out there. Our challenge is to help those restless souls find their rest in Christ.

Rational argument itself will seldom start an unbeliever on the path of being pulled toward the magnetism of Jesus. That is much more likely to happen through the pull of relationships with believers who know Jesus and demonstrate the quality of life he offers. Ultimately the work of calling to belief is done by the Holy Spirit. He works, of course, through presentations we do of God's Word about our relationship with him and the centrality of Christ's reconciliation.

Some Basics of Church Growth

Ultimately it is the Holy Spirit who calls people to faith and gathers them together as a church. But he works through people and relationships. How do we do our part? Let's get practical.

Church Growth studies can provide a framework for such discussions. The discipline of Church Growth was developed at Fuller Theological Seminary during the years I was vice president and faculty member there. Two names stand out. Missiologist Donald McGavran laid the foundation. C Peter Wagner popularized his concepts. Through unusual circumstances, I became Mr. Church Growth in my church body. I still have pastors thanking me for my insights and advocacy that freed them up to do innovative ministry.

The basic principle about which all agree is that a congregation has to want to grow and be willing to make difficult decisions that facilitate intentional growth in size. Such a conscious setting of priorities was not needed in the peak years of mainline denominational growth during the migration to the suburbs. Such churches mostly grew from within and by attracting members who already knew their church culture well. Those years are gone.

Most of the congregations in mainline church bodies are in decline. Is there a will to make growth in size a high priority? Where is the leadership in setting a new priority over against maintaining traditions? What kind of fine-tuning of old church cultures will be officially encouraged for the sake of more effective outreach?

The Homogeneity Principle

Second most basic is the homogeneity principle. People like to go to church with others like themselves. That's demonstrated in the history of immigrants who gathered with those speaking the same language. Their grandchildren typically could no longer speak it and drifted away. Typically, the third and fourth generations grew up in the suburbs and have greater affinity to young adults like themselves who share the suburban lifestyle of family, schools, homes. Many growing community churches have tapped into that new culture.

Churches with their roots in a special language-based ethnic culture are prone to have a defensive posture over against anything that is not traditional. But those immigrant years are generations ago. We face a new homogenous culture, especially in the suburbs. Thank God for a polity that allows congregations to develop their own worship styles as long as they remain within theological boundaries. My experience is that pastors who have "gone contemporary" gladly embrace the traditional theology.

Church Growth Diseases

Peter Wagner was the most visible advocate of Church Growth principles. He taught the Fuller Seminary D.Min. course on Church Growth that enrolled a large number of mission-minded pastors from traditional denominations. I would meet with each group and hear their relief that it was finally OK to talk about practical ministry issues.

Among his principles, Wagner would use a congregational life cycle to highlight certain diseases. Two are fatal. One is ethnikitis, in which a congregation tries to maintain itself in a community that has changed. Unless they develop new ministries targeted to the changed community, they will sooner or later fade away.

Fatal also is old age. This may affect churches in dying communities, as is happening in many rural areas where everything is shrinking. It also happens in churches with a remnant that simply age out. They have not had the energy or leadership to try new ministries. The end is in sight when they no longer have the resources to afford a full-time minister. In my district, roughly 40% are at that point.

When the end is in sight, congregations can react two ways. Most typical is a sense of failure and guilt. They have been unfaithful and let previous members down. But the reality is they faced powerful sociological changes that overwhelmed them. Better is to celebrate all the ministries done when the congregation was healthy. I have advocated for years the development of a hospice program for churches at their end. Go out with dignity. Celebrate what has been accomplished by this congregation over the decades.

What to do with the property? Here is a radical suggestion. Give the buildings to a young congregation that has growth potential, even if it is not from the same heritage. Carry on the basic mission through a biblically sound church with a culture better attuned to the current community.

Liturgical Worship

The worship wars in many denominations wound down about twenty years ago, with the two sides firmly in place. A fresh perspective is offered by C. Kirk Hadaway, writing from a Southern Baptist perspective. He notes that the presence of "liturgy" is more characteristic of plateaued churches than growing ones. "Research shows that formality and liturgy are often barriers. Plateaued churches need excitement and life, and it is hard (though not impossible) to wed formality with excitement."

Whether worship should be exciting is a controversial issue in highly liturgical churches. But the topic here is church growth principles. Something has to be exciting enough to bring visitors back again.

Spiritual Maturity

Hadaway acknowledges that if he would revise his well-known book *Church Growth Principles*, the one key principle he would add is prayer. Church Growth leader Peter Wagner, I know from first-hand experience, was a man of intense prayer.

Overall, according to Hadaway, there is an increasing recognition of the importance of spiritual depth for a congregation to grow. He cites research from five mainline denominations showing that churches characterized by a greater emphasis on spiritual development also tend to be growing congregations. "Millions of Christians want spiritual depth in their lives, and they are not finding a way to grow in many mainline and conservative churches in America. People are seeking churches which can provide an opportunity for spiritual growth, and when one exists, the word spreads quickly."

The Holy Spirit's Power

My overall theme is that the Holy Spirit does the calling, gathering, enlightening and sanctifying of God's people. We can and should do common-sense things that expand the number of contacts with those who are not connected to Christ. But churches of Christ are not just another social organization out trying to recruit new members. We have something distinctive to offer. We offer the Spirit, who brings his power to bear on the lives of Christ-followers.

Turning around a declining congregation is very difficult. There are no guaranteed methods. What frustrated pastors can do is concentrate their efforts on developing spiritual growth among those already assembled. Teaching the Word is basic, of course. But there is a difference between teaching and the learning that happens. More on that later in discussing the process of Spiritual enlightenment.

Facilitating personal spiritual growth is an intensely personal and time-consuming process. It is done best when led by pastors who are themselves growing closer to God by the power of the Spirit.

Organizing a Fellowship of Christ

Martin Luther gave us the wonderful description of the four-fold functions of the Holy Spirit. This Third Person of the Trinity calls, gathers, enlightens and sanctifies God's people. The previous five essays reflected on how the Spirit calls people into a relationship with Christ. These next five focus on how the Spirit gathers believers to live and work as a fellowship of Christ.

I live in Broadview Heights, Ohio. It is a community of 20,000 residents living in 7,700 households with 5,250 families. The community elects leaders who form the Broadview Heights government. The purpose of City Hall is to serve the residents by providing police and fire protection as well as garbage pickup. At election time the community residents get to evaluate how well its officials are serving them. The City Hall of Broadview Heights is doing a great job, recently finding funds for a new Recreation Center without raising taxes much.

This basic distinction between community and governance has been confused for most of church history. The formal institutionalized structure has considered itself the church. But in New Testament thinking, the spiritual action is in the underlying informal fellowship, the community. That's where the Holy Spirit works. Poor church governance can actually become a barrier to healthy spiritual fellowship.

In the decades after World War II, many congregations opted to structure themselves like social organizations such as the Red Cross, the Elks Club or the American Legion. These emphasized recruiting volunteers and getting them involved through an extensive committee structure. Too often the result was confusion and apathy. I once had the opportunity to visit a number of pastors in what we call circuits of about ten churches. I inquired what their basic problems were. By far, most said, We can't get anybody to do anything!

Basically, they were suffering from a poor understanding of the Paul's theology of church. Their heritage led them to think of the decision-making structure as the church that counts. That's because the Medieval heritage focused on a separate class of Christians called clergy, distinct from everybody else, called laity (the people). The clergy do the ministry; the laity support them. This tunnel vision caused the historic denominations to completely miss Paul's teaching on the ministry gifts that all participants bring to church, as he explained in 1 Corinthians 12 and Romans 12.

The Misunderstanding of the Church

Theologian Emil Brunner explained the basic problem in his book *The Misunderstanding of the Church*. He was addressing the ecumenical movement of the 1950s. Impressed by what large-scale war production and troop movements accomplished in the Second World War, the major Protestant church bodies dreamed of what they could accomplish if they merged together world-wide. Delegates met frequently to work out compromises and mergers. But they had little to show for all their efforts.

The problem, Brunner observed, is that what they were trying to organize was not the real church. They were dealing with the formal structure of delegates representing their various denominations. Denominations in turn represent the governance structure of the congregations that make up that church body. All that superstructure is not the real church, pointed out Brunner.

The basic unit of Christian churches is the fellowship of believers gathered around and applying God's Word. These can remain quite informal. They can be a handful of participants working together to further a ministry. It is in these primary relationships that the Spirit is most active and most readily works. Church governance structures are one or several steps removed from the real action.

Spiritual Energy

What makes Christian churches unique is their dependence on the presence of the Holy Spirit. Otherwise, they can become just another social organization out recruiting volunteers for social service projects. It's the Spirit that provides the unique human energy of a healthy congregation.

We live in a world where the main source of human energy is the services that money can buy. I like to read about business plans for growing a company. In today's economy, if you are not growing, you are in decline. Is that true also for churches? Business growth happens by developing new products and finding new markets for them. Crucial is hiring people with the talent and energy to successfully bring the product to market. That takes money. This usually means borrowing in various forms. Then the race is on to succeed before the funding is gone.

Churches cannot buy their way to success with money. They can and do raise funds to support ministries and build buildings. But the first step is to touch hearts and increase allegiance among those gathered as a congregation. That's ultimately the work of the Holy Spirit, and he can't be bought.

Ministry and Governance Structures

Administrative wisdom lies in recognizing and developing two forms of church organization. Call one the *governance* structure of respected leaders charged with making decisions about property, finance and policy. Call the other the *ministry* structure of participants actually doing ministry and supporting each other in primary fellowships. The job of the second-level governance structure is to guide, shape and protect those doing the primary-level ministries.

The problem that frustrated those pastors who could not get anyone to do anything is that their congregations had adopted a committee structure that looked good in theory but brought confusion and apathy. They fashioned an outline of what an ideal congregation should do, usually drawn as boxes with detailed prescriptions of duties and meetings. Then annually a nominating committee would recruit members to fill those boxes, sometimes presenting a slate of 50 or more people. The weakest link in this paper organization was the individual motivation of those who agreed to do their duty. An added weakness was the confusion resulting from overlapping responsibilities.

Missing from this committee structure, adopted from social organizations, was provision for motivation to do what the box prescribed. The appeal was to do one's duty as a loyal member of the organization. Too often the recruitment appeal came with the promise that the individual won't have to do much. The resulting apathy is predictable.

I once served on a church evangelism committee and remember well the moment when we all realized we were giving directions for what someone else should do without knowing who that person was. None of us saw ourselves doing the work. The result? Nothing got done beyond what was already happening. We had just added confusion.

Instead of fitting members into boxes outlining duties, a better way is to think about organizing support for those who are individually motivated to do specific kinds of ministries. First comes the Spirit-driven motivation of individual believers. This is where pastoral leadership is crucial. Then comes developing structure to support their work.

But what if no one steps forward to do a ministry? Then that won't get done. The church has to wait until the Spirit motivates someone to do it. Focus leadership efforts on the primary task of fostering Spiritual growth. Then there will be new energy to organize.

A basic lesson I learned in years of church ministry is to not waste the time of those who are moved to do ministry. Don't ask them to sit spend hours in planning meetings. Get them right to work. Let them figure out how to organize to better accomplish what they want to do.

They did not know it at the time, but those pastors who could not get anyone to do anything were facing a Spiritual problem. That's because they were working with a theology of church that made little recognition of the central role of the Spirit in church life today.

Gathering a Spirit-Shaped Congregation

Eugene Peterson is well known as the translator of the Bible paraphrase *The Message*. I had the privilege of joining him in a conference small group addressing the issue of the relationship between spirituality and church administration. His position was simple. There isn't any. He started his ministry as the pastor of a suburban Presbyterian church. He was blessed to have others who took care of the well-established administrative routines of running the congregation, while he focused on personal spiritual growth.

Peterson's simple position is attractive. But as an organizational theorist, I disagree. The issue is complex. The formal structure of a church is a tool that is used poorly when the goal is just to keep the basic routines of church life going. It is used well when focused on shaping relationships through the spiritual growth that can happen in the underlying fellowships of those gathered.

The Congregation As Topsoil

In his book *Under the Unpredictable Plant*, Peterson offers an arresting image of church life. Think of those gathered as the topsoil for the Spirit's work. The topsoil is "the material substance in which all the Spirit's work takes place—these people, assembled in worship, dispersed with blessings.

"They are so ordinary, so unobtrusively there, it is easy to take them for granted, to quit seeing the interactive energies, and to become so pre-occupied building my theological roads, mission constructs, and parking lot curricula that I start treating this precious congregational topsoil as something dead and inert to be arranged to suit my vision.

Why do pastors so often treat congregations with the impatience and violence of developers building a shopping mall instead of the patient devotion of a farmer cultivating a field?"

This image of topsoil builds on the very first parable Jesus told, the Sower and the Seed. Some seed fell on soil that was hard, rocky and weedy and produced a poor crop. Others fell on the good soil that yielded a bumper crop. Church leaders do well to concentrate on that good topsoil where it exists in a congregation. Paul continued the image when he regarded the Corinthians as a field where he planted the seed, Apollos watered it and God gave the growth (1 Corinthians 3).

Peterson observes, Our pastoral work "is not to make a religious establishment succeed but to nurture the gospel of Jesus Christ into maturity. Holiness cannot be imposed; it must grow from the inside." He cautions against working in generalities. "When I work in the particulars, I develop a reverence for what is actually there instead of a contempt for what is not, inadequacies that seduce me into a covetousness for someplace else."

Everyone Is Given the Manifestation of the Spirit for the Common Good

Paul was a missionary for the fourteen years between the start of his first missionary journey and his first imprisonment. He stayed in Ephesus for over two years—long enough to be a pastor and watch what developed out of his preaching the Gospel. He drew on those observations in his writings to the troubled church in Corinth. He worked from the conviction that the Holy Spirit, Christ's Spirit, was central to the life of new fellowships of Christ that emerged from his work. In 1 Corinthians 12 he explained the spiritual foundations of church life.

First, no one can say Jesus is Lord except by the Spirit of God. This same Spirit provides the energy for ministries done through a fellowship. Such energies are a gift. In individuals such gifting looks like natural talent and acquired skills. These talents become a gift to the fellowship when the Spirit moves individual members to offer them in ministry to others. Here is the key phrase: "To each the manifestation of the Spirit is given for the common good."

The Spirit moves many to contribute financially to the common good. Talking about money in church can be uncomfortable, especially when approached as just raising dollars to cover the bills. But the Spirit can change individual priorities for spending available personal funds. Then contributions can move beyond duty to opportunity for growth. The Spirit likewise manifests himself when teachers step up to provide that form of ministry. The same goes for those who are encouragers and leaders.

I am drawing on a list of gifts from Paul's letter to the Romans written after observing what was happening in the Ephesian and Corinthian congregations. The Corinthian listing included unusual gifts like speaking in tongues, doing miracles, and prophesying. We in traditional churches don't know what to make of those gifts. The later list in Romans has manifestations that any congregation would be glad to have in their life together.

Revolutionary View of Ministry

Many churches inherited a faulty church organization that divided the congregation's work among committees with prescribed duties and meeting times. The obvious unasked question is what would motivate members to take on such jobs. The assumption was that members would do this out of loyalty to their church. But such institutional loyalty is disappearing in traditional churches. No wonder little gets done beyond what a faithful few continue to do.

Paul's approach to ministries is revolutionary in our times. He was describing what actually happened, not just prescribing what should be done. Key, of course, is the Holy Spirit, who was the motivator of all the fellowship life Paul observed and advocated. In his Trinitarian blessing to the Corinthians, Paul stressed that the distinctive of the Father is love, of the Son is grace. The contribution of the Holy Spirit is the fellowship life of Christ's church. Lose sight of the underlying informal fellowship, and you diminish the importance of the Spirit at work in church relationships. Then the care and feeding of the institution became more important than the care and feeding of the fellowship.

Administering Spiritual Gifts

Peter, too, understood spiritual gifts as the basis for ministry. "Each should use whatever gift he has received to serve others, faithfully administering God's grace in its various forms (1 Peter 4: 10). Such administration is an organizational task for which some are especially gifted. Like a match maker, find out what members enjoy doing and do well. Then find opportunities in congregational life for them to serve.

A Spiritual Gifts Inventory is a basic tool to do the first part. These usually offer about a hundred questions probing what the respondent likes to do and does well. These are basically conversation starters and do not meet the standard of psychological tests with high validity and reliability. As I understand the history, such inventories are only about forty years old.

Erik Rees offers a set of tools to help individuals in a congregation discover how they would like to contribute to the ministries of a congregation. His workbook is entitled *S.H.A.P.E.* It promotes discussion of an individual's personal **S**piritual gifts, **H**eart, **A**bilities, **P**ersonality and **E**xperiences. It is meant for use by small groups. Its purpose is accomplished when each concludes, Yes, this is me. Key is the Heart as the seat of passions. The congregation's job is then to help each member live out their Spirit-induced passion to use their giftedness in ministry to others.

But application of spiritual gifts administration causes a new problem. How do you find enough roles so members can do what the Spirit has gifted them to do? Healthy churches solve that with good organization and administration. Such engagement over time will outpace congregations that can't find enough people to do even basic ministries in a downward spiral of loss of energy.

Ministry by manifestation of the Spirit for the common good is so very biblical. Centuries of traditional institutional church life produced a blind spot to how to reenergize congregational life.

REFLECTION 28

Reducing Barriers to the Spirit's Work of Building Fellowship

"If you want to build a ship, don't summon people to buy wood, prepare tools, distribute jobs, and organize the work. Rather, teach people to yearn for the wide, boundless ocean." Antoine de Saint-Exupery

My book *Builder Ministry For The 21ˢᵗ-Century* offers many dimensions of church administration that can be gained from management perspectives. It keyed off the Apostle Paul's self-identification as the master builder of the fellowships of Christ in the churches he oversaw. At the time, I had not invested much attention to understanding the central role of the Holy Spirit in Paul's approach to ministry and leadership.

The Holy Spirit calls, gathers, enlightens and sanctifies God's people. He is the energy that drives ministry. To use a sailing analogy, the Spirit is the wind that fills the sails of the ship of congregational life. Our job is to hoist the sails and avoid making mistakes that would slow down movement or even cause the congregational ship to flounder. What we need is a Spirit-centric approach rather than a human-centric focus on what leaders can and need to do. The Spirit does the work. How do we avoid quenching his fire?

Natural Church Development

Christian A. Schwarz offers such a perspective in his work on *Natural Church Development* (www.ncd-international.org). Start with the kingdom of God as God's reign in our hearts through the Holy Spirit. Recall Jesus' parable of the growing seed in Matthew 4. "A man scatters seed on the ground. Night and day, whether he sleeps or gets up, the seed sprouts and grows, though he does not know how. All by itself the soil produces grain." That's what can happen through the basic ministry of presenting God's Word in creative ways. Remember, "I (Paul) planted the seed, Apollos watered it, but God made it grow."

Decades ago, the frontier of the new perspective on managing churches was to carefully formulate goals or outcomes and perhaps to do a business school analysis of Strength, Weaknesses, Opportunities and Threats (SWOT). By now, such purpose statements are common in well run organizations and churches. The problem for churches is that we don't control the wind that moves the ship. A popular pastor of a large well-run church caught my attention with an article he wrote on "Why I Don't Set Goals." He didn't because Spirit leads the church into the future. Our job is to follow as well as we can.

Christian Schwarz gathered self-evaluation data from over 1,000 congregations of all sorts of backgrounds. Thirty members each assessed their congregation according to eight categories called qualities of church life. Their scores were interpreted as average, below average and above average. It turns out that churches with mostly above average qualities also were growing in numbers. The data show that church quality drives quantity.

I highlight here four qualities that are especially Spirit-related: Passionate Spirituality, Inspiring Worship, Gift-oriented Ministry, and Empowering Leadership. The question for church leaders is, What are we doing that brings us up short in one or another of these qualities? How can we remove barriers? Where can we improve the ways we unleash the Spirit in our midst?

Passionate Spirituality

According to Schwarz, "The secret of growing churches is definitely not found in their particular style of spirituality (charismatic, non-charismatic, liturgical, non-liturgical, etc.) but in the level of passion at which faith is lived out among the members." The question is whether the spiritual life of the members is characterized by prayer, enthusiasm and boldness.

Prayer life may be strong among individuals in old, mainline congregations. But it is typically not very visible. Our heritage teaches us not to be passionate, because passions can lead astray. Our history uses feelings of guilt as a motivator, but guilt brings only short-term results without passion. "Instead," as Schwarz advises, "work to develop a 'culture of appreciation' in your church. Be a good model."

Inspiring Worship Service

Schwarz: "All parts of a church service, from the seating arrangements to the music and to the message, should become more and more the vehicles through which the Spirit of God and God's love can be experienced in the community of Christians." These "vehicles," of course, need to be Christ centered, grace focused as well as Spirit shaped.

When the Spirit is at work in a gathering for worship, there is excitement, refreshment and a sense of new possibilities. Can the Spirit work through the same routine from week to week among believers who attend mostly out of habit? Certainly, in theory. Greater appreciation of what's missing, however, can come from listening to the experience of visitors and also from visiting other congregations. Experienced observers of healthy congregations note how they convey a sense of excitement and anticipation for the Sunday event.

The Holy Spirit works through relationships centered on the Word. In general, the more people involved in leading the worship event, the better; each offers a different touchpoint. The more the sermon applies the Word to everyday relationships among those gathered, the better. The more the music is accessible to others beyond just the veterans, the better. The more attention is given to improving the worship experience, the better. My own conclusion from a lifetime in highly structured services is that the more informal, the better. In general, reduce barriers to the Spirit by increasing emphasis on Word-centered relationships.

Gift-Oriented Ministry

According to Schwarz, if your church finds this quality characteristic of gift-oriented ministry below average, it does not mean that your workers are doing 'bad' work. Rather, it indicates the work in your church is not oriented enough to the passions and abilities of its members. Your church may be relying on duty rather than the Spirit to motivate. The concept of spiritual gifts plays a central role in all the other seven quality characteristics. What is at stake here is nothing less than the very character of the body of Christ gathered in a specific place at a specific time. View a congregation as the topsoil for the Spirit's work. Recognize that the Spirit wants to move into action participants with specific interests and talents.

What if you don't have the right combination of gifted ministers for what you are hoping to accomplish? Then you pray that God send the right person. In the church plant I did, we lost our drummer. For over a year and a half we prayed for a new one. In God's own time, he sent us a professional drummer.

Empowering Leadership

All Spirit All the Time does not remove the need for human leadership and wisdom. Spirit-gifted ministers need structure and support. Paul's overview of spiritual ministries includes administrators and leaders. Those so gifted can figure out how to help others perform their tasks by setting goals, offering guidance where necessary and providing technical assistance. They learn how to create a feeling of approval, recognize individuality, and provide fair treatment.

Congregations know when they don't have good administrative leadership. There is a pervading sense of confusion which can cause frequent conflict or result in apathy. Some pastors can provide such leadership themselves. Most aren't so gifted. They need to appreciate and allow for someone who can provide guidance. Wise congregations can provide for a ministry coordinator to work alongside the pastor.

The goal in a Spirit-driven congregation is to reduce barriers to his work. Find the biggest barriers in a specific church and work creatively to reduce them. Let the Spirit guide those efforts.

The Limits of Rule-Making in a Grace-Focused Congregation

Henry Schwan was a highly respected pastor of a large Lutheran congregation in Cleveland in the latter half of the 19th century. For fifty years he faced thousands of German immigrants who were attracted to the opportunity to carry forward the culture they knew from the old country. He despaired that so many approached church life as a set of requirements for belonging and participating in the congregation. He criticized this legalistic attitude.

In a conference presentation to other pastors *(Concordia Theological Monthly*, 1945), Schwan contrasted this attitude with a Gospel-based approach to life together in a congregation, which he summarized as an evangelical attitude. He knew how to distinguish between Law (legalistic) and Gospel (evangelical), based on Paul's contrast in Galatians 3.

"Evangelical practice treats everything in evangelical fashion. This means that we expect justification before God, the renewal of the heart, and the fruits of the Spirit only through the Gospel. In everything we do we have this one thing in mind, to give free course and sway to the Gospel."

When Schwan talked about evangelical, he meant grace-focused. We are saved by grace (the Gospel) not by works (legalistic expectations). An Evangelical approach does not make the state of grace dependent on keeping the Law or meeting behavioral expectations.

In his presentation Schwan was speaking to mostly second-generation pastors of what was essentially a Pietist emigration to the new country. He was challenging them to appreciate their roots in what was an even earlier Pietist movement. Those roots emphasized the Spiritual motivation for new life in Christ. But such personal evangelical motivation does not transfer over well to later generations. As that happens, church life degenerates into rule-keeping prohibitions against un-pious behaviors like dancing, gambling, attending theater or movies. Generations grew up confusing the Gospel with living out rules for behavior.

I experienced the extremes of that approach when attending a church school where the dean tried to shape student behavior with a fifteen-page rule book prohibiting any kind of behavior that could cause problems. My favorite was no throwing snow balls with a stone in them. There were more rules than anyone could possibly keep in mind. The book was a joke, especially in the hands of a dean of students who swore at students to whip them into shape. He exemplified extreme legalism.

Evangelical Motivation

Johann Arndt was the grandfather of the Pietist movement. He presented a healthy perspective on the balance between grace-oriented and legalistic ministry.

"True knowledge of Christ is ignited by the Holy Spirit in our hearts as a new light that becomes ever brighter and clearer. A man is newborn in his conversion if the righteousness of Christ is given to him through faith. Then the image of God will be daily renewed. He is not yet, however, a perfect man but a child who must yet be trained by the Holy Spirit and day by day become conformed to Christ Jesus."

This movement shifted from legal to biological language and from external to an internal work of God. It placed a heavy emphasis on growth—growth in knowledge but also growth in grace. The intent of the movement is captured in this phrase: "God is not only good enough to justify persons, but he is also powerful enough to change them."

Evangelical Disappointments

As a pastor addressing other pastors, Heinrich Schwan wanted them to be prepared for disappointments in pursuing evangelical practices. Such practices should flow from knowledge of the Gospel, *but do so rather seldom and slowly.* Evangelical practices expect the fruits of the Spirit to be produced solely by the Gospel and *is willing to wait for them.* Such practices *bear with all manner of defects, imperfections and sins* rather than remove them merely in an external manner. Evangelical pastors will resist letting fiery zeal become legalistic practice. They will avoid overabundantly castigating individual sins. They will not engage in unnecessary, unedifying polemics.

Schwan warned that an evangelical attitude will resist making large the chasm between those who are in and those who are outside the congregation. Evangelical pastors will build bridges toward those on the outside. The Gospel is a gift, not an accomplishment. It is to be shared widely rather than restricted only to those who show enough appreciation for it. The instinct is to give the Gospel away to the many rather than hold tightly among the few.

Bridging from Cultural Faith to Convicted Faith

Heinrich Schwan was facing members attracted to church through a shared immigrant culture. They had a cultural faith. He was holding out for convicted faith. A social culture is the beliefs, values and behaviors passed from generation to generation. The reality is that most members in church cultures stay focused on behaviors and thus try to regulate them, usually placing a high value on legalistic expectations. The beliefs are usually left to authorities to define, which they do by teaching Bible truths and faith based on them. Too many merely assent to these beliefs rather than personally owning them.

The inherited culture Schwan faced did not place a high value on moving head knowledge to heart conviction, beyond describing what that should look like. Indeed, that old culture resisted distinguishing between those who have "real" faith and everybody else. Such emphasis can bring resentment from those who remain "normal" believers. That old church culture placed a high value on avoiding divisiveness.

Moving beyond cultural faith to personal conviction is like a conversion. Whether cultural faith saves for eternity is not the issue. That end-of-life outcome is offered by grace to all who confess Jesus as

Savior. Rather it is a conversion to a new growing personal relationship with God and to new motivation to become more like Christ in personal values and behavior.

This change comes only by the work of the Holy Spirit. Beyond presenting the Gospel as creatively as possible, we cannot put the Spirit on a schedule or demand that he do what we think is necessary. In the quaint nineteenth-century phrase, we have to "give free course and sway to the Gospel." It is this reliance on the work of the Spirit that can be so frustrating to pastors looking for quick results.

The Problem of Later Generations

Churches that have mostly cultural faith face the problem of the later generations. Will young adults continue in the ways of their parents? The present reality is that most don't. The old church culture is dying.

Of course, the pressing issue is what to do about bringing new generations back into church life. The only real solution is to increase exposure to the Spirit's work through the Word. It's not going to happen by trying to enforce rules that are easily ignored. It is only going to happen through creative grace-focused, Spirit-shaped ministries.

Fine-Tuning Your Congregation's Culture

Do not quench the Spirit, Paul admonished the Thessalonians. The context makes clear he is talking about their behavior as a gathered fellowship. Respect those who work among you. Encourage the timid. Be joyful. Whatever you do, don't put out the Spirit's fire. The contrast is fellowship behavior that unleashes the Spirit in their midst. As Paul wrote to Timothy, do fan into flame the gift given you.

There are behaviors congregations can do that end up quenching the Spirit. A big one is having such rigid relationships that the Spirit can't gain much traction to help individuals recognize their personal giftings to contribute to the common good. Peter urged his people to "faithfully administer God's grace gifts in their various forms" (1 Peter 4: 10). The opposite is to be negligent in such organizing and encouragement. Such was the case in pastoral leadership until recent generations. The old way did work. It doesn't anymore.

How do you change the behaviors of a congregation in ways that more faithfully unleash the Spirit and fan into flame the work he does to motivate fellowship members? You do that by sending better messages of what members and their congregation can become.

Four Sources of Messages on How to Behave in a Congregation

When I was teaching Organization Behavior, the whole point was to improve the performance of those working in an organization. I used a scheme that analyzed the sources of messages that determine what a person actually does on the job. The objective is to improve the messages that count.

David S. Luecke

1. *Formal* Messages are mostly expectations put into writing, like policy statements and job descriptions. In churches these can be doctrinal formulations and vision statements. They are important to have but don't actually change much behavior in themselves until they are reinforced with other kinds of messages.

2. *Informal* Group Messages interpret what is really important in a congregation's life together. What does a newcomer see others actually doing or routinely ignoring? Consider what they talk about after the formal service. Do they reflect on the sermon and worship? Do they share experiences with God? Or is theirs the small talk that can be found in any social setting?

3. *Technique* Messages shape so much of what workers actually do, like now working from home in front of a computer screen with Zoom communication. Churches employ many kinds of techniques for shaping their life together. Is prayer done mostly by the pastor reading written words, or is it done informally by many? Is the order of service taken from a hymnal or presented more informally on a screen? Is the music done with an organ or a praise team? Churches have their unique cultures recognized as customs, which themselves are accepted techniques. Change techniques and you are in the process of changing the culture.

4. Action Messages are what participants find themselves actually doing. Words have turned into action. Does a church care enough about the action of serving others to organize events that actually get participants involved in service projects?

Such action messages are the most influential in shaping behavior, while written formal messages are the least. Most traditional churches assume the top-down approach and too often never get to action messages.

If you want to more open more pathways for the Spirit, change what participants actually say and do. Move beyond just preaching about it.

A Few Principles for Changing Organizational Cultures

In business, the culture of a corporation is a huge topic these days. The intent is to introduce changes that will increase productivity or some other outcome necessary for the organization's continued success. Edgar Schein authored the classic analysis in *Organizational Culture and Leadership*, a text used in business schools. He explains how corporate cultures tell their members who they are, how to behave toward each other and how to feel good about themselves. If these basic functions are true in a business, think how much more they apply to a church, which is all about providing basic identity, values and moral foundations for behavior.

- Recognize at the outset that changing a culture is anxiety provoking. Some will lose what they have valued and resent those who seem to be gaining. When we remodeled the sanctuary, the architect suggested that we replace the red carpet with a green one. Upset about other changes going on, a member of the Altar Guild became so angry that she flung the green carpet-swatch clear across the sanctuary.

- A second principle is that strong leadership is needed to bring about organizational change. Without leaders that advocate change, congregations will settle back into what is familiar and comfortable. The key leader, or course, is the pastor, who decides what to feature and who functionally has veto power over initiatives of others. Pastors typically have their core expertise in the ways of the old culture. Few are prepared for the difficult task of negotiating changes to new practices with which they themselves have little experience. Leadership for change is easier if other leaders are ready to understand and support.

- Culture change inevitably brings conflict between those who like the old and those espousing the new. By personality, most pastors are inclined to avoid conflict if possible. Leading change necessitates skills in handling conflict.

Earning the Right to Change a Culture

- Leaders have to earn the right to be followed in new behaviors. In Edgar Schein's words, "Whatever is proposed will only be perceived as what the leaders wants. Until the group has taken some joint action and together observed the outcome, there is not yet a shared basis for determining whether what the leaders wants will turn out to be valid."

- Culture changes through shared experiences of success. It makes sense to earn credibility by starting with relatively small changes that are easy to make and are welcome by almost all. Negotiating easy changes will build trust.

- Culture trumps vision. Vision is about ideas. Culture is behavior. Culture change is all about turning new ideas into action that past behaviors would resist. Historic churches stress beliefs. Behavior consistent with beliefs is now more important.

In short, until words turn into successful actions, not much will change in a declining church. Preaching and teaching a new emphasis is a good start, especially when it is rooted in Paul's theology of church and ministry. But until words result in action, persistence on that theme can turn into nagging that annoys more than motivates.

Sometimes a growth spurt in a congregation is preceded by an "igniter" event. Often unplanned, such an event allows the congregation to experience success, which brings about new energy and openness to change.

One church I know of took on a service project of cleaning up the city park nearby. A TV crew came to interview them and produced a segment on the evening news. With this visible success the leaders were then ready to put more energy into exploring new ideas for ministry.

Getting Switches Turned on for Enlightenment by the Spirit

The Spirit's job is to call, gather, *enlighten* and sanctify God's people. The focus now is on how the Spirit enlightens with his gifts. Many church leaders fall into the trap of assuming their ministries are primarily their job to accomplish with their own gifts and abilities. Then they too often become disappointed when the results aren't what they expected.

Paul expanded the enlightenment concept farther by asking that "the Father give you the Spirit of wisdom and revelation, so that you may know him better and that the eyes of your heart may be enlightened (Ephesians 1: 18). The Spirit of wisdom enlightens hearts as well as heads.

To "illuminate" is another word for the enlightenment process. It offers the image of a light bulb turning on. Houses typically have a 200-amp service box that brings electricity in from the outside. The box then routes the energy across 20 to 40 circuits to the various rooms and appliances throughout the house. To enlighten a single light bulb, the main breaker and the appropriate circuit breaker have to be on. Some individual light switches have a dimmer, which can be set for low lighting or turned all the way up for full brightness.

By analogy, the electricity is, of course, the Holy Spirit, who delivers power to the "eyes of the heart." In ministry, what flows through the wire is Christ-centered biblical truths. Just learning the words brings low-level, dim lighting. But when Luther focused on people being enlightened with gifts of the Holy Spirit, he had in mind more than reciting biblical truths. The Spirit wants to brighten hearts and excite passions.

How does that happen through ministries of a church? What actions can we humans take that make it easier for the Spirit to touch hearts and turn bulbs on bright? Can we identify things we do that get in the way of the flow of Spiritual energy, that keep the switch turned low?

Getting Past the Age of Enlightenment

Enlightenment is a heavy word in our Western culture. The Age of Enlightenment was a movement in the 18th century in reaction to "unreasonable" church dogma. Reason based on evidence was to prevail in making life's decision. Thomas Jefferson was a leading exponent who enshrined the Enlightenment values of "life, liberty and the pursuit of happiness" in the American Declaration of Independence. Famously, he edited the Bible to leave out references to irrational miracles and the supernatural.

Ever since that Age, Christian churches have been struggling with issues of faith and reason. American Protestantism is divided between those churches where reason prevails and supernatural miracles are explained away, on the one hand, and, on the other, churches that maintain a biblical worldview. My own observation is that those who have gone "scientific" are swiftest in decline among church bodies.

Until recent generations, resistance to Enlightenment was associated with ignorance. But now about half of high school graduates go on to college, half of them graduate and half of those go on to earn advanced degrees. The scientific approach to life is well understood and appreciated. Yet there is a widespread and growing hunger for more, for the supernatural God and his supernatural ways. This means an increasing openness to the extra-ordinary Holy Spirit and his extra-ordinary ways of enlightenment.

Moving Beyond the Medieval Model

One of the least effective ways to turn on Spiritual enlightenment switches is the religious education approach that goes back a millennium. Medieval teaching focused on the Trivium. Start by learning grammar.

Then learn logic. Put these two together then in rhetoric—the art of persuasion based on logic. These were the beginning lessons, followed by the upper-level Quadrium: arithmetic, geometry, music and astronomy, all of which are logic oriented. Much less than one percent of the population would then go on to university studies in one of the three branches of theology, medicine and law. Academic theology focused on reasoning about interpreting Scriptures and logical principles for understanding divine truth. Scholastic debates were about whose logic could prevail, and those were sometimes conducted like a sport of one-up-manship.

This commitment to logic continued in catechisms for training children in church beliefs. These took the format of questions and answers. The most prominent were Luther's Small Catechism and the Heidelberg Catechism for those in the Calvinist tradition. In my heritage, doctrinal teaching in general was done with a proof-text method of stating the doctrine and proving it with three or four Bible passages. Being inquisitive, I found that many of those texts were, at best, only tangentially related to the truth being taught. The attraction of this method was the appearance of logic.

Unasked in this traditional approach to teaching was what the students were learning about living the Christian life. For most, they learned the importance of getting the words right when talking and thinking about God. With that came reluctance to say anything about their faith lest they get the words and logic wrong. The light switch to Spiritual enlightenment was on, but the bulb remained dim. Was the bulb on bright enough to receive eternal salvation? In a grace-focused church, the answer has to be yes. Yet a Spirit-shaped church has to hold out the hope that through the Spirit's gifts the believer's bulb will burn more brightly to illuminate a more God-pleasing life.

There Is a Better Way

This medieval approach only poorly addressed what we know today as personal motivation. Is logic alone a good motivator of the desired behavior? Is it true that all you have to do is to explain clearly what and why someone should do something, and they will agree to change their behavior accordingly? Sometimes. But this would usually be for behavior about which the person does not have a strong personal opinion or preference. Where feelings are strong, the power of logic is weak.

Reflect on Peter's encouragement, "Just as he who called you is holy, so be holy in all you do" (1 Peter 1: 15). The logic is clear. But is this statement persuasive? Will it change behavior? It may for those who are already motivated by the Spirit to please God out of love for him. But that already assumes an advanced state of Spiritual enlightenment. Logic itself only poorly motivates love, the emotion fundamental to the Christian life.

What are some better ways to prepare the way for the Spirit to bring more of his special enlightenment to those who are considering or already know Christ? With logical truth in the background, Spiritual truth is ultimately a relationship with God. That grows best through encounters with believers who already know him and share their life experiences.

The Spirit can work especially well among those experiencing a life-crisis that shakes their self-confidence, such as the death of someone dear, or losing a job, or the defeat of a life ambition. Those settings are switches ready to be turned on by the Gospel conveyed in a loving way.

Jesus taught that where two or three are gathered in his name, there he is with them. After his Ascension, he is present with us now through his Spirit of enlightenment.

Finding More Switches for Enlightenment

Spiritual Enlightenment happens when switches get turned on. Ministry is all about finding those Spiritual switches that work for people at their various ages and situations in life.

Our first-grade daughter came home from school one day and skipped around the house shouting "I can read. I can read." Something had clicked that day. Now she could associate visual symbols with the sounds she associated with meaning. She grew up around books that were read to her. She became an avid reader.

I have talked with reading specialists who describe their method of helping children sound out alphabet letters and associate them with pictures, like a cat or a dog. They describe special moments when it all "clicks," and children take off in their readings. But for some the "click" does not happen, and reading remains a laborious process done only slowly and reluctantly.

The reality among adults is that finding the right switch for Spiritual enlightenment depends on where the individual is in his or her life and how they process information. Each brings unique personal experiences into an encounter. I learned long ago that when I am preaching a sermon, I am preaching 150 sermons to the 150 in attendance. My words have to snag their attention wherever their thoughts are at the moment. Many come worried about family problems, or are nursing grudges or are anxious about their health. Words I use can mean many different things to those processing them. My words need to be engaging and practical. I need to gain and hold their attention.

Truth As Encounter

Emil Brunner is a mid-20th century theologian who had a great influence on my thinking through two books. One is *The Misunderstanding of the Church*, where he demonstrated that informal fellowships of the Spirit are the church that counts, not the institutional forms of the day. The other is *Truth as Encounter*, where he unpacked the limits of truth statements in doctrinal propositions about God. The truth that counts is a relationship with God through encounters with him.

All seminary-educated pastors take a series of courses on Christian teachings about basic topics like the Father, Son, Church and End Times. Naturally, we think these truth statements are the way to know God. In actuality, they offer only truths *about* God. The Bible teaches that God is a person, not an abstract truth. He is best understood in the person of Jesus Christ, who calls us into a relationship with him. We can describe those relationships, but that is not the same as experiencing Christ-centered relationships with God. Therein is the dilemma for ministry. We can and should logically teach about God and describe the desired relationship, but actually featuring and modeling encounters is more effective for Spiritual enlightenment.

My suburb has a sign encouraging drivers to "Believe in Broadview Heights." I often puzzle what city leaders want to convey in their message. I think they mean to have hope that great things will happen in our town. This would be good.

As a verb, to believe means to trust. It's hard to trust an abstract concept. Trust describes a relationship of confidence in good intentions of someone I know. For me, that sign brings reflection on how I can trust God as he has revealed himself in the Person of Jesus Christ. I can know and describe Christ as an abstract notion. My life takes on new meaning when I learn to trust Christ as a friend who brings new meaning into my life. Those moments are the work of the Holy Spirit.

Faith (trust) and hope are two of the three basics of the Christian life that Paul presents at the end of 1 Corinthians 13. The third is love. Love is the ultimate relationship term. My encounter with the loving

God invite me to respond to him in love and to extend his love to others around me. Loving encounters are what the Christian faith is all about.

Martin Luther's Encounters

Martin Luther was unique among theologians of his day. He had a very personal relationship with God. It first expressed itself when he was overwhelmed in a frightening thunder and lightning storm that he took as the voice of an angry God. He responded by joining a monastery.

A scene In the 2003 film *Luther* stands out for me. He was in his monk's cell physically wrestling with the devil, bouncing off the walls. The spiritual realm was up close and personal. Luther deeply feared God. That's why when later the switch turned on that illuminated justification by grace through faith, he felt a great personal experience of relief that his works were not necessary.

The other great Reformer a several decades later was John Calvin, founder of the Reformed Presbyterian church, from which modern-day Evangelicals are descended. A perceptive, highly trained lawyer, he expressed biblical truths in the impersonal terms of a law book, the *Institutes of the Christian Religion.* Centuries early, the great Catholic theologian Thomas Aquinas wrote volumes of logical propositions about God. The story is told that one day he had a profound personal experience, and he never wrote a word again.

Luther is unique in that he remained a Bible scholar who felt no compulsion to turn biblical insights into an integrated system of logical declarations about God. That he left to his good friend Philip Melanchthon, who was followed by later generations of systematic theologians. In the early years of the Reformation Luther had profound respect for the Holy Spirit, who had done so much to him. Later rational theologians did not know what to do with the Spirit beyond a few generalizations, so they mostly left him out of their systems.

Classical Protestant theology can be expressed as a system of proposition like those of Calvin. Or it can be appreciated as a series of personal discoveries and convictions about how God interacts with his people. In today's culture, Luther's legacy will fare better than Calvin's.

I and Thou

Very formative for Martin Luther was his relationship with his monastic mentor and Confessor Johann von Staupitz. He later remarked, "If it had not been for Dr. Staupitz, I should have sunk in Hell." He had developed a relationship with a superior who was kind and caring enough to challenge him to move beyond his overwhelming fear of God. For him, the face of God had been his stern and demanding father whom the boy Luther could never satisfy.

In the relationship between Luther and Staupitz, a switch turned on that helped transform him through the renewing of his mind. Brilliant scholar Luther knew all about the God of the Bible. A major enlightenment occurred in his study of Romans as he pondered "the righteousness *of* God." The grammar allowed translation as also the righteousness *from* God. His world started to change when he realized that righteousness was something God gave him, not just demanded of him.

What happened can be explained in terms of the distinction between seeing God as an "It" or as a "Thou," as offered by Martin Buber. The "It" is an abstraction that does not bring a personal response. The "Thou" is a person one enters into a relationship with. For many, God remains an "It," that is above and beyond them and needs to be feared and revered. The Holy Spirit's work of enlightening turns the "It" God into the loving "Thou" God to whom we want to be drawn closer.

Ministry today needs to do better at finding switches the Spirit can use to move personal enlightenment beyond recitation of biblical truths.

The Case Study Method for Spiritual Enlightenment

By far, the most popular degree in colleges and universities is business administration. It is very practical and seen as the gateway to a better job and pay.

I did my M.B.A right after graduating from seminary. The contrast was breathtaking. Seminary was mostly theory and history with only the most obvious application. Business school was practical application with only the most relevant theory. I did the M.B.A. to learn how better to organize church life.

My pastoral career has been a time of wrestling with seminary-type church theory and result-oriented practical ministry application. If something is not working, why do we continue to do it the old way? Why aren't we trying out new and better methods?

My years teaching Organizational Behavior in two business schools consisted of looking for more and better practical experiences or cases that could be analyzed in the classroom setting. This approach was pioneered by the Case Method of the Harvard Business School. Cases are essentially stories about people making a decision. The best cases don't have an obvious answer. Always the emphasis is on what students are learning, not just theories being taught.

Case Studies in Spiritual Enlightenment

The ministry issue at hand is what we can do to ease the way for the Holy Spirit to bring Spiritual enlightenment to those seeking God. My instinct is to highlight cases of how real people have experienced God in their personal lives. We have case stories of the experiences of people in Bible times. Good preachers and teachers are able to make those classic cases come alive for people today so we can reflect on how to apply them to our lives now.

But what about cases of people living here and now in circumstances like ours? These can add persuasiveness to the Bible message applied to lives today. Such cases can illustrate how the Spirit changes lives today and build anticipation of what he can do in my life, too.

For years I attended a monthly breakfast fellowship of Evangelical men at a local restaurant. The feature each time was someone sharing his personal born-again story. Evangelicals can become quite proficient at telling their personal story, with entertaining details and practiced punch lines. I would leave encouraged and praising God for what he did in that particular life.

One of the men from our Lutheran church plant worked up the courage to tell his own story. I was disappointed. He was not a good story-teller, because he had never done this before. What I noticed by the end is that his story was mostly highlights of his church life. He was not talking about a personal relationship with Christ. Church was a stand-in for his relationship with God.

I noticed the same orientation when I was interviewing candidates for a facility manager. One of the job qualifications at the seminary was that this person be a Christian. Some told their born-again story. One could name the date of his encounter. Two others were from mainline denominations. One of those explained that he sang in his church's choir. The other was an usher at his church. The church culture they grew up in let the secondary experience of involvement in church activities substitute for a primary relationship with God.

The Missing Chapter on the Holy Spirit

A good case study leads to reflection on the more general theory involved to provide guidance for understanding similar experiences. In church life, that theory about God and man is called doctrine. At the core is understanding the Trinity of God the Father, Son and Holy Spirit. In my seminary doctrine text there is a curious lapse that took me years to discover. The first volume of such dogmatic texts is usually on the Father, the second on the Son. Logically, the third would be on the Holy Spirit. But there is no chapter on the Spirit. This third volume jumped right to sanctification. What happened to the Holy Spirit? Who is he? What does he do?

Reformation heritage focuses on what God has done in Christ. But it has a blind spot to what God is doing in lives today, beyond inference that the resurrected Christ will do today what he did in the Bible times. In those Reformation years, the Holy Spirit was a dangerous topic because he could lead astray those who claimed a direct experience, as happened in the calamity of the Peasant's Revolt in 1525. Safer is to let the church interpret biblical truth and how God relates to humans.

The fundamental issue in theory is whether God does indeed directly speak to and interact with believers here and now. This overarching issue comes to the surface in the question of whether or not God does miracles today, defining a miracle as an extraordinary event for which there is no natural explanation. A positive view is not to be found in classical Reformation theology, which typically claims that miracles no longer happen after Bible times.

Yet eighty percent of Lutheran pastors acknowledged they have experienced or witnessed a miracle, as defined above. Such is the outcome of a large-scale research project I did. Survey results are a modern way of reporting individual case stories. If God can intervene to bring a cure that is otherwise unexplainable, he through the Spirit can plant thoughts in the minds of those seeking him.

Another way is to recognize the Spirit at work is by sharing whisper stories of believers who experienced a sudden urge to visit someone or do something "right now," and something faith-affirming results. Every discussion group I have led has one or two examples. That insight opens the door to broader discussion of experiences of the currently active Spirit changing people today.

The Theory of Experiential Learning

David Kolb is a psychologist whose theory of learning is popular today. He states that styles of learning can be analyzed along several dimensions. One is whether the individual prefers to generalize from concrete experience or to first learn abstract generalizations that are then applied to specific situations.

Traditional seminary-trained pastors learned through a *deductive* process, starting with principles and maybe getting to application. Enlightenment by the Spirit happens best, I think, with an *inductive* process of moving the opposite way from specific experiences to generalizations. How much could ministry be improved if pastors had exposure to business school-style case analysis in their own learning process? Many pastors of growing community churches do indeed have a business background and even a business major. They are oriented to concrete experiences.

I recognize this newer direction in the preaching approach Pastor Andy Stanley, Jr. writes about in *Communicating for a Change*. He starts by mentioning an experience he has had and suggests maybe you have had it, too. Then comes what the Bible says. The flow goes to how I have tried to apply it in my life. You can try it, too.

What the Bible says remains central. But this approach focuses on case studies of concrete experiences. In a sermon, there are limits to case specifics that can be featured. But the possibilities in other church settings are limitless. One thing I have noticed over the years is that the attention level of participants goes up significantly with this kind of story-telling.

Do you want the Gospel to have greater impact on people's lives? Start with specifics, then add reflection and theory. Is the old approach of starting first with biblical theory easier? Definitely. But that leads to the question of how important it is to be effective in your ministry. Which approach can be best used by the Spirit to touch and change lives?

Lifelong Enlightenment by the Spirit

All churches took a heavy hit to their church attendance during the Covid season of 2020-2021. Typically, in-person attendance dropped by a third to a half. Video streaming enabled some to participate from home. That's good, but is it as good as being together in one room, joining in praise and sharing informally? Will involvement go back to pre-pandemic levels? As of this writing, a clear trend to recovery is not evident.

What a challenge to church life. There is something deep in most preachers that wants to scold members to come back. The writer of Hebrews verbalized that approach. "Let us consider how we may spur one another on toward love and good deeds. Let us not give up meeting together, as some are in the habit doing, but let us encourage one another (10:25)." Shaming people back to church may have worked a little in former times. But don't expect much response to that approach today.

I have talked to more than a few life-long church attenders who, post-pandemic, explain that going back to church just isn't important to them anymore. They did not miss it. Their habit was broken. I myself have had a season subscription to the symphony for over twenty-five years. I have not renewed it. I found that I did not miss it.

If, indeed, going to church is in the same category as going to the symphony, the future is not bright for churches that rely on traditions. What's the answer? The pressure is on now for churches to demonstrate that they offer something beyond what other cultural institutions can do. We need to demonstrate how church life really does spur one another on toward love and good deeds, and that participants are really encouraged by one another.

Offering Lifelong Enlightenment Through
Spirit-Oriented Relationships.

What churches can offer is lifelong enlightenment by the Spirit. It is the presence and power of the Spirit that makes church life compelling. The Spirit's work is renewal, making things fresh again in a believer's relationship with the Father and the Son. Renewal happens through fresh encounters with the Word as conveyed through others. It's the Christ-centered, Spirit-powered relationships that make church life special.

Paul summarized for the Colossians what happens when they gather together, " Let the peace of Christ rule in your hearts and be thankful" (3:15). We can read this as a command. Better is to hear it as an expectation for what can happen in their time together. Does it? Do those who come experience peace with God and a refreshed sense of thankfulness for his blessings. If not, why come again?

Inquiring about personal thankfulness is a good starting point for reaching out to those who no longer attend. Reaching out is indeed a basic function of a well-led congregation. I recall the complaint of a man who had been very active. He noted that when the church wanted something from him, they figured out ways to contact him. But nobody seemed to notice his absence and apparently no one cared. Resentment is not a good base for rebuilding a relationship. Much better is a reminder of the opportunity to express thankfulness for God's blessings in their lives.

Paul continued that when the Colossians gather, "you teach and admonish one another with all wisdom." To admonish can be heard as to scold. Who wants to go to church to be scolded? A better translation is to remind. Go to church to be reminded of what you believe. To teach can mean to present facts. But for long-time members there are typically not many Gospel-related facts they have not heard. But that is only one kind of teaching. Broaden the concept to include the teaching of one another through sharing life experiences. What have others learned in their walk with the Spirit that can spur one another toward love and good deeds? That's part of Spiritual enlightenment.

Spiritual Songs

Paul rejoiced that the Colossians "sing psalms, hymns and spiritual songs with gratitude in your hearts to God." How to do that in today's rapidly changing culture is a challenge. Singing long-established hymns led by a pipe organ still works (for a while) with older church goers. Singing with contemporary instruments, rhythms and phrases makes sense for younger church goers.

But some cautions are in order to lead singing that comes with gratitude in the hearts of those participating. Much of contemporary music is played too loud and is too performer-oriented. For singing to be a fellowship event, people have to hear each other, and that's hard to do with loud amplification.

When alternative music began emerging in the 1980s and 90s, it was named contemporary in contrast to traditional. That naming was unfortunate in the implication that the songs are ever changing to keep up with whatever is the latest on Christian radio. But to be truly spiritual, songs need to be sung with soulful conviction. That happens only with familiarity. Some Boomer music is good enough to be song by later generations. Sing for the audience gathered at that time and place, not for a hypothetical audience of twenty-somethings.

Virtual Church Fellowship

One new form of ministry I pursued with much effort and many dollars I called Virtual Church Fellowship. It was a specially formatted web-based program inviting members' discoveries about their faith. These would be written up and submitted first to an editor who would assure the contributions were faith affirming rather than complaints. To help participants recognize their experiences worth sharing, the site had lead questions according to three categories: Faith Insights, Reactions to Church Emphases, and Spirit Sightings. During development, I solicited written comments that were truly exciting and contributed to Christ-centered fellowship.

But I finally had to abandon the project. Here is what I discovered.

Most people don't like to think out and write up their insights. They are much more willing to share their thoughts orally with spontaneity. This can be done now with making short videos. But my technology was too outmoded to facilitate that. While it is easier to initiate Facebook Groups for sharing among participants, these exchanges too often remain shallow.

Perhaps someone with more tech savvy will get and develop the vision of orally sharing faith experiences without being in the same room together. That's the heart of the kind of church fellowship the Spirit wants to build.

What Will the Future Bring?

One easy way to view the future of Christian churches in America is to project current trends out 25 or 30 years into the future. The result looks grim. Traditional churches now have mostly older adults who in time will pass on to the next life. They are not being replaced by younger generations. The problem with this simplistic approach is the underlying assumption that the conditions which shaped the last twenty years will remain the same for the next twenty. The 2020-21 Covid pandemic wrecked almost all the projections of businesses and governments. Unexpected things happen.

Hope for a better future for Christian churches in American comes in several forms. One is that God reigns supreme, and the Spirit is very active calling and gathering a growing number of believers in other parts of the world. Broad Spiritual awakenings have happened in America in the past. God could do it again. The field of those looking for a better life is ripe for harvest. Pray for fresh movement of the Spirit. That is more likely to happen through fresh church forms that are more friendly to the Spirit.

The Spirit Calls, Gathers, *Enlightens*,
and Sanctifies God's People

Keep Trying Innovative Ministries

The cues people respond to today are different from those of even thirty years ago. Think cell phones and social media. Churches have always been a source of cues for recognizing and reacting to God. What's happening today is that the old cues are not bringing expected responses. Thank God for church leaders willing to try innovations to be more effective in their ministries. Some of those changes may not work out well in the long run. But such efforts can bring valuable excitement. To be effective in mission to others in a changing world is to be constantly innovating.

In my lifetime, I have seen a major innovation among Lutherans that, judging by results, has not worked out well. This was the introduction of an increasing amount of formal ritual into worship. In the decades after World War II, the slogan was "Liturgical Renewal." The introduction of liturgies going back centuries provided excitement at the time. But such innovation, in my opinion, has not worn well over time. I will be strongly criticized by others in my church body for saying this, but I think highly formal liturgy is associated with stagnant and declining church life today. It was a wrong turn.

The issue came into focus for me when I did a funeral-home service for an elderly member. My message featured a review of salvation by grace and immediate presence with God in heaven. A week later I received a call from the daughter scolding me for offending her Catholic friends. They apparently expected an inoffensive ritual of familiar words. I delivered a personal call to the biblical Gospel.

My negative reaction to the liturgical renewal movement may stem from my personality. But I think it has biblical footing. Rather than *liturgical* renewal, ministry revolves around *Spiritual* renewal and how best to present opportunities for the Spirit to bring newness to the hearts of those reached.

Keeping the Sacraments Personal

Greater reliance on the sacraments was basic to liturgical renewal. But I worry that increased ritual has weakened their effectiveness. Baptizing can be done with a pages-long liturgy. Better it is to informally talk through what needs to happen for an infant to be baptized and raised in the faith. The church I serve has an annual Reaffirmation of Baptism on the second Sunday in January for the Presentation of Jesus. The font is moved front and center. One by one participants come forward down the center aisle. The pastors dip their finger into the water, make the sign of the cross on the forehead and say, "This is to remind you of your baptism in the name of the Father, Son, and Holy Ghost." Almost all eagerly participate and I can see anticipation in their eyes. It is a very personal, meaningful experience for them.

Preparation for Communion

The liturgical renewal movement brought more frequent practice of the Lord's Supper. The goal was every service, and the norm now seems to be twice a month. What got lost is special personal preparation for the experience of receiving Christ's body and blood.

The 19th century congregational practice of communion had much to offer. It was celebrated four times a year. Each time was an occasion for special personal preparation. The parish pastor made the rounds to visit each family to offer counsel about what was happening in their lives. Personal relationships were deepened. Then the preparation process got simplified when communion moved to once a month and the telephone became widely available. My memory as a child in a parsonage is answering the phone to hear a parishioner "announce" they were coming to communion that Sunday. Presumably they were spiritually prepared. Even that specialness has now disappeared. When distributing communion, I often wonder what is going on behind the eyes of those at the communion rail. Has partaking in the Lord's Supper become just a ritual without much personal content?

Pastors can work hard to make the application personal by explaining the symbols. But why not just make the Gospel personal without the extra layer of the symbols and ritual? In practical terms, the more time spent on distributing communion, the less time for preaching the Word in an hour-long service. The recommended sermon length has been reduced to twelve minutes, with the rationale that people now have a short attention span. But the better solution to that problem is to make sermons more effective at holding attention with good illustrations and application to contemporary life.

Confirmation

The practice of confirming boys and girls in their faith has been around since the earliest centuries of the Christian church. In my personal experience Confirmation was a big cultural event, bringing a new suit, a watch and my own Bible with my name inscribed. The big hurdle was Questioning before the whole congregation, where we confirmands had to demonstrate our knowledge of biblical doctrine. Stress was high. The assumption was that head knowledge somehow equates with Spiritual condition.

Over recent decades I have watched as resources for confirmation have expanded, particularly through the work of Rich and Arlyce Melheim and their Faith Inkubators material. Gifted educators, they focus on offering many touchpoints that can engage participants, drawing them into discussions of what their relationship with God can mean to them. Significantly, the curriculum describes their themes as "Head to Heart." Old timers may criticize that there is too much emphasis on fun. But at issue is whether these youth will see church as a valuable resource for reassurance as they encounter the difficulties of life ahead. The loss of younger generations certainly raises questions about the effectiveness of customary ways of raising children in the faith.

One innovation lies in the direction of exposing confirmands to older "graduates" like themselves who have felt the hostile pressures of high school and college and come out with their Christian commitment even stronger. Hearing such "success" stories can be very affirming.

The Alpha Course

When I focus on innovations in ministry, I mean biblically faithful changes that are acceptable in a traditional mainline congregation. Be open to what growing Evangelical community churches are doing. In my experience, most of those churches are biblically sound. I don't think it necessary to denounce them for not taking the sacraments as seriously as my heritage does. These are supplements to the basic Gospel.

The Alpha Course has much to offer. By now over 30 million have participated. Originating out of an Anglican Church in London, Alpha is basically a simple eleven-week Bible study that offers fellowship in a meal, a Bible-based presentation on basics of relating to God and a small group discussion. It is oriented to newcomers who are exploring the faith. It presents itself as *Real* where participants can be authentically themselves, as *Relational* where friendships can form and *Reliant* on the Holy Spirit "because we realize that it is only God who changes people—we just introduce him." I offered Alpha seven times at my church.

What makes it Alpha special is the half hour video presentation by Nicky Gumble, senior pastor at Holy Trinity Brampton. He is a very accomplished, humble speaker who holds attention well and is not at all "preachy." What he offers that no one else can equal is case studies of the experiences of previous participants in Alpha. A special Saturday five-session focus is on the Holy Spirit, what the Bible says about him and how he changes lives. The tone in the course is that something special is happening, and this is reinforced with the frequent stories of changed lives among participants. Expect change and it will more likely happen.

Shifting the Starting Point for Thinking About Our Relationship With God

In Martin Luther's words, "Through the church the Spirit gathers us, using it to teach and preach the Word. By it he creates and increases sanctification, causing it daily to grow and come strong in the faith and in the fruits of the Spirit." Sanctification is a *process*. Elsewhere he teaches that "Now we are only halfway pure and holy; the Holy Spirit must continue that work in us."

Sanctification is also a *condition*. Paul addressed his readers as the saints, the sanctified ones. Through Christ's redeeming work, they were already holy and set apart before God. In the final judgment we will appear as fully sanctified in Christ.

Those in the Reformation heritage understand well the sanctification as a *condition*. We have not done well on the *process* of being drawn closer to God and growing in the fruit of the Spirit. The fundamental issue in the Reformation was the role of good works in our relationship with God. The key discovery was that our works do not justify us before God. Sanctification is not justification, to use the key categories of that debate. But you can't make progress with just negatives.

After I had preached a sermon on new life in Christ, the office received a complaint from a visitor that I had preached on sanctification, and "Lutherans don't do that." I understood where this stalwart was coming from. But what a strange view on ministry that we can't emphasize how to live the Christian life. The purpose is not to win God's favor to get into heaven; Christ already took care of that. Today a hunger for "getting into heaven" is no longer prevalent in our current society. But there is great hunger for the fuller, more abundant life in this world.

Restructuring the Issue for Our Times

Sanctification is a hard term to grasp. It's "churchy" and seems distant from everyday life. Paul gives us a better handle. In Ephesians 4: 13 he urges that the body of Christ may be built up until we "reach to the very heights of Christ's full stature." To the Corinthians he explained that we "are being transformed into Christ's likeness with every-increasing glory, which comes from the Spirit" (2 Corinthians 3: 18). To become more like Christ is the goal of sanctification. It conveys movement from far away to very close. Such growth provides practical goals for ministry.

Gordon D. Fee offers a major restructuring of how to understand sanctification. He is one of the pre-eminent New Testament scholar of our day. I was fascinated by his lengthy book *God's Empowering Presence*, his detailed study of the Holy Spirit in the letters of Paul. He identifies 169 such references and explores each. What gripped my attention was the final Part II Synthesis, which I had to re-read many times to absorb his reasoning. His categories were compelling because they are drawn directly from Paul.

Shifting the Starting Point

The Reformers focused on the conditions of justification and sanctification, and, for all practical purposes, they left the Spirit off to side. In Paul's world, the Spirit is the starting point for theologizing about the Christian life. According to Fee, "The Spirit is not the center for Paul—Christ is, ever and always—but the Spirit stands very close to the center, as the crucial ingredient of genuinely Christian life and experience. For this reason, the Spirit arguably must play a much more vital role in our rethinking Paul's theology than tends now to be the case."

The primary reason Paul's approach to the Christian life is different from that of the Reformers is that Paul addressed believers who had directly experienced the Spirit in their personal lives. The Spirit was a living presence for them. In subsequent generations and centuries, most Christians were born into the faith. That's why infant baptism became so prevalent in Catholicism and persisted in traditional mainline churches. In those traditions, there is no previous experience of the Spirit to appeal to. Such experience does not justify us before God. But it does demonstrate God's power to change our lives and give us new zeal for living in Christ.

A common view is that God does not come to us directly but he does that through the church. This explains why the third volume of my dogmatics text starts, not with a theology of the Holy Spirit, but with a description of sanctification by the Spirit, which is accomplished through the Christian Church. There is no reference to personal experiences of the Spirit.

Fee explains, "Westerners are instinctively nervous about spirit activity, be it the Spirit of God or other spirits; it tends not to compute rationally and is therefore suspect. Hence our difficulties with regard to any genuine 'restoration' of the experiential life of the early church."

We might want to say that Paul's experience of the early church is irrelevant to churches in the Reformation tradition. But how dare we!! He is God's apostle for God's church. Our alternative to dismissal is to become more discerning in spotting that evidence of the Spirit's work in our personal lives. In T. S. Eliot's phrase, "We had the experience but missed its meaning."

The Spirit Produces Fruit

What took me many re-readings of Fee's Synthesis is how he bases the new life on the fruit of the Spirit in Galatians 5: 22-25. He cites the fruit of love, joy, peace, patience, kindness, goodness, faithfulness, gentleness and self-control. These are samples of what the Spirit produces in believers. Then comes the simple appeal, "Since we live by the Spirit, let us keep in step with the Spirit." The sanctified life consists of walking with the Spirit.

It takes three shifts in thinking to appreciate Paul's starting point. One is that he addresses what the Spirit does rather than who he is. Second, he is not describing the conventional virtuous life. Third, these fruit are essentially feelings or experiences imparted in us by the Spirit.

Scholar Lorenz Wunderlich broke new ground in the traditional understanding when he wrote on the Holy Spirit in the 1960s. The title, *The Half-Known God,* is an acknowledgement of the blind spot in our heritage. Significant to me was the discovery that in this 110-page book there are only two paragraphs on the fruit of the Spirit. Also significant is that the ministry gifts of 1 Corinthians receive only one paragraph. Rediscovery of such gifts is truly revolutionary for ministry today.

The subtitle of Wunderlich's book is *The Person of the Holy Spirit.* He addressed who the Spirit *is*. In contrast, Luther wrote about what the Spirit *does*; he calls, gathers, enlightens and sanctifies. That question of what, rather than who, is more productive for guiding ministry today.

The Pauline Perspective Is Better Than the Reformer's Categories

Here is Gordon Fee's conclusion to his synthesis and application of Paul's theology.

"In sum, I for one think the Pauline perspective has the better of it: and I also believe that perspective can become our own—dare I say, "must" become our own, if we are going to make any difference at all in the so-called post-Christian, post-modern era. But this means that our theologizing must stop paying mere lip service to the Spirit and recognize his crucial role in Pauline theology; and it means that the church must risk freeing the Sprit from being boxed into the creed and getting him back into the experienced life of the believer and the believing community."

Spiritual Journeys of Growing Closer To God

The Pilgrim's Progress by John Bunyon has been a great classic of spiritual literature for centuries. It tells the story of Mr. Pilgrim's journey to the Celestial City. On the way, he encounters many detractors but also many encouragers. What makes this journey very appealing is its reliance on allegories that are symbolic fictional figures and places

My personal interpretation is to see those who encourage Pilgrim as believers who exemplify the fruit of the Spirit at work in their lives, such as the characters Faithful, Hopeful, Goodwill, Mercy, Prudence, Charity and others. Recognize their parallel to the Spirit's fruit of love, joy, peace, patience, kindness, goodness, faithfulness, gentleness and self- control.

Think of your life with God as a journey. Your ultimate destination is the Celestial City in eternity. In this life, what's the next step you aspire to in being drawing closer to God? In Paul's terms, what more of Christ's full stature will you reach for? In Luther's terms, where would you like to see your new nature in Christ become stronger and what of your old sinful nature would you like drowned out.

Greater sanctification is not something you achieve on your own. In Paul's terms, "Since we live by the Spirit, let us keep in step with the Spirit." In Luther's terms, "Now we are only halfway pure and holy; the Holy Spirit must continue that work in us."

Use the following chart to draw out your personal Spiritual journey. Where are you now in your relationship with God? The left side of the chart represents being close to God or far from him at various stages of your life. The bottom line presents those stages, starting with your childhood through youth to the present. Plot your personal history. Key is where you want to be in the future. A typical believer's chart would be a line curving upward from left to right.

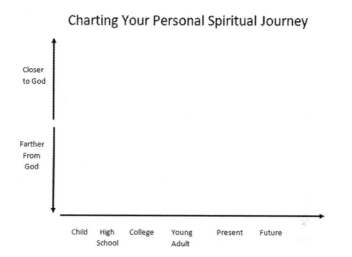

Charting Your Personal Spiritual Journey

In traditional Reformation thinking, infants at baptism are close to God, and they get closer through years of education leading to confirmation. Until recent times, the chart would then show a straight level line from left to right into the future because there were few social challenges to the faith as received. Now, of course, high school and then college present many challenges to confirmation faith, so that the line for many young adults dips farther from God and stays there. But some do come back, especially when children come along. Those reading this are probably looking to become closer to him.

Think through your personal journey of closeness to God. Dwell on individuals who helped or hindered you on your version of Pilgrim's Progress. You might want thank those encouragers you associate with helping you discover more hope, joy, peace and patience on the way.

Luther's Three Stages of Faith

Martin Luther offered a three-stage model of growing closer to God. It is found in a sermon preached in 1521. Using the analogy of a sanctuary, he described a church-yard conscience concentrated of getting the rules of church life right. A nave (pew section) conscience characterizes those who are living faithfully but out of guilt with no joy. Progressing forward, those who are living with a heart changed by the Spirit have a chancel conscience.

Here is Luther's ideal stage: "When the Spirit comes, he makes a pure, free, cheerful, glad and loving heart—a conscience made righteous by grace, seeking no reward, fearing no punishment, doing everything with joy."

What if Christian churches became known as centers of joy where people are making progress toward pure, free, cheerful, glad and loving hearts? Those congregations would be attractive to so many in our mixed-up world where few have lasting experiences of the joy available in Christ.

Recognize Four Stages of Faith

I offer a four-stage model that expands Luther's understanding of progress in sanctification. Mine divides the middle nave stage into two, distinguishing between cultural faith and convicted faith.

Call the initial stage Merit-Based Faith, living by the rules. It is characteristic of children. But many adults never get beyond this Stage One in their faith life. I was once teaching lay pastors when one wanted to know if it's OK for a Christian to smoke. I stopped the class and led a long discussion of salvation by grace. When he came back the next day, I asked if he thought smoking was something a Christian could do. His answer? No, that's not right. His thinking was stuck at the childish Stage One.

Stage Two is Cultural Faith, a faith held in common with others in a shared culture. Confirmation is acceptance into the church faith. It is a good way to live, as long as it is not challenged or no longer seems popular. Traditional Cultural Faith is now under stress. It is not being passed on well to the next generation.

Stage Three is Convicted Faith when a believer has taken on ownership of the personal faith. Cultural faith confesses, "I believe what the church believes." Convicted faith confesses, "This is what I believe and by which I will live my life."

Stage Four is Close-to-God faith, as so well described by Luther as living joyfully with a glad and loving heart. Let that be the aim of every personal spiritual journey.

Stages Three and Four are the Spirit's work. They are not a human achievement. The challenge for traditional churches is to better prepare the way for the Spirit to move believers along.

Such a journey moves beyond the basic question of saving faith. Salvation belongs to all who confess Christ as Lord and Savior, even if they do not understand well the implications. Jesus did teach that unless you receive the kingdom as a child you will not enter it.

Greater Christlikeness Through Church Life

"Now we are only halfway pure and holy," says Martin Luther in his explanation of the Spirit's work of sanctification. "Holiness has begun and is growing daily." (*Large Catechism*, Third Article). So many of us in today's world are trained to measure and assign numbers to what we are working with. Wouldn't it be great if we could quantify sanctification? Then we could measure progress. If I am halfway there now, what will three quarters of the way look like?

Dr. Seuss's *How the Grinch Stole Christmas* is a classic. There is an animated movie version. The Grinch's problem is that his heart is two-sizes too small. His experience in Whoville proves life-changing. His heart grew three sizes. The video version has a magic X-ray screen that shows Grinch's heart growing inside his chest.

Wouldn't it be great if we had a magic X-ray at the entrance to a sanctuary so we could get a measurement of how big each person's heart is that day? We could put those measurements into a big data bank along with other measurements of that person's involvement in the congregation.

But be careful what you wish for. Our human nature would want to turn those numbers into competition for who is holier than someone else. Thus we could end up feeding pride, whereas basic to the progress of sanctification is growth in humility.

Research on Moving Closer to Christ

But what if some numbers could be put in the service of improving the ministries of a congregation? That possibility is attractive to me as a former business school professor. What could we do better to help participants move along on their personal journey to becoming closer to Christ? We all have the basic data of church attendance. But that can reflect things other than spiritual maturity. Growth in quality is certainly possible without quantitative growth.

A research team associated with Willow Creek Association tackled that issue of what can be measured in church life so that a congregation can improve its ministries. Their publication is *Move: What 1,000 Churches Reveal About Spiritual Growth*. They carefully developed a questionnaire that 1,000 churches distributed to their participants.

Among their conclusions: "Yes, there actually are ways to know whether the people in our congregations are truly growing more in love with God and extending that love to other people. Yes, there are churches among us to are experiencing significant authentic spiritual growth within their people. Yes, there really are ways to measure changed hearts. Yes, there are lessons we can learn, attitudes we can incorporate, successes we can emulate, and spiritual-growth milestones we can help our congregations reach."

Their questionnaire sought feedback from church participants on Spiritual beliefs and attitudes, Personal Spiritual practices, Organized church activities, and Spiritual activities with others. Based on the answers of 6,000 respondents, they divided them into four groups. Those exploring Christ, Growing in Christ, Close to Christ and Christ-centered. What attitudes, practices and activities were associated with growing close to Christ?

The researchers clarify that spiritual growth is not linear and predictable. It is determined by each person's circumstances and the activity of the Holy Spirit. But there are patterns.

Differences Between Exploring Christ and Christ Centered

For spiritual *attitudes*, less than 30% of the church participants in the first stage of Exploring Christ reported that "I exist to know, love and serve God, I desire Jesus to be first in my life, and I love God more than anything else." For those in the fourth stage of Christ-Centered, those attitudes go up to ninety percent. That's a three-fold increase.

The spiritual *practices* surveyed are: reflecting on Scripture, daily confessing my sins, studying the Bible to know God, praying daily for guidance, setting aside time daily to listen to God. Ten to twenty percent at the first stage do these practices. At stage 4 two thirds pray daily for guidance and study the Bible. Half pray daily to confess sins. That's roughly a four-fold rate of growth.

The data show a five-fold rate of growth in willingness to risk everything in my life for Christ, feeling fully equipped to share my faith with non-Christians, recognizing that supporting God's work is my first priority in spending money.

What do answers to these questions reflect? They are as close as we can get to measuring progress on the journey to becoming Close to Christ and then Christ-centered. Basic is the belief that such growth is driven by the Spirit interacting with individuals in their various life situations. The responses are reflections of hearts that have grown three (or five) times bigger.

Church Support for Personal Spiritual Growth

Another part of the REVEAL Spiritual Life Survey inquired about the help each respondent wants from their church to support them in their spiritual growth. Appreciate the boldness of this approach. It is basic to the challenge of church leadership today.

The data show that for those who are starting their spiritual journey the worship experience and a sense of belonging are very important. Both are at the core of being a congregation that reaches out to others. For those well along on their spiritual growth, these are replaced by the challenge and encouragement to grow and take next steps in personal responsibility for spiritual growth.

For congregations with long-time church members, I propose that the challenge is first of all to highlight the importance of progress in sanctification, or becoming more like Christ, highlighting what it is and why it is important. That's a big first step. Then would come the creativity of figuring out challenges for greater growth and how to encourage that.

Church Leadership Take-Aways

Here are several of the researchers' conclusion about what leaders can do to support spiritual growth of those in their congregation:

- Realize that church activities themselves do not predict or drive long-term spiritual growth. They have the greatest influence in the early stages of such growth, but then personal spiritual practices become more important.
- Nothing has greater impact on spiritual growth than reflection on Scripture. Make the Bible the main course of the message. Help participants commit to fitting Bible and prayer into their busy schedules. Model Scripture as the church's foundation.
- They key attribute of the pastor is an unrelenting, uncompromising drive to help people grow into disciples of Christ.
- Make the destination clear.
- Make participation in spiritual growth basic to the church's purpose.
- Make the senior pastor the champion.

Note how the pastor(s) are key to helping believers grow in sanctification. They can and should develop programs that challenge members to grow in the Spirit. But most effective for the growth of others is what they personally model in their own spiritual life.

The Pietist Impulse for Evangelical Ministry

Sanctification is the journey of being drawn closer to God. It is not an accomplishment we achieve on our own. The Holy Spirit is the key actor.

What is our part in the process of sanctification? Verbs become important. Some would say that we decide to follow Christ. But that implies our changed relationship with God is something we accomplish. Then we lose sight that our special relationship with him is a gift by his grace. Theologians warn against the danger of "synergism"—working together.

What is a better verb? Try "to invite." Our part in this grace-focused relationship is to put ourselves where the Spirit can most readily work on us. Use the image of the Spirit's workshop. That is wherever believers are gathered around God's Word and sharing its meaning in their lives. A church building readily comes to mind, where the Word is preached and applied, and people sing their praises. But the Sprit's workshop can also be where two or three are gathered in Christ's name discussing the practical implications of their special relationship with God.

My Heart—Christ's Home

Robert Boyd Munger uses the image of rooms in our house where we can surrender our natural sinful condition to the Spirit's influence. He challenges us to invite the Spirit to change our perspective on how we live. His immensely popular spiritual guide is *My Heart—Christ's Home,* most readily available in a small booklet published in 1986. Munger was a Presbyterian pastor who taught at Fuller Theological Seminary and developed the spiritual formation program in which I became a mentor.

Munger keys off of Paul's word to the Ephesians "that God may grant you to be strengthened with might through his Spirit in the inner man, and that Christ may dwell in your hearts through faith (Ephesians 3: 17). He offers the paraphrase "That Christ may settle down and be at home in your hearts by faith." Another foundation is John 14: 23: "If anyone loves me, he will obey my teaching. My Father will love him, and we will come to him and make our home with him." A third reference is Revelation 3: 20: "I stand at the door and knock. If anyone hears my voice and opens the door, I will come in and eat with him, and he with me." Note the verb "to open" the door. That's our part of the sanctification process.

Here is Munger's interpretation. "If you want to know the reality of God and the personal presence of Jesus Christ at the innermost part of you being, simply open wide the door and ask him to come and be your Savior and Lord. After Christ entered my heart, in the joy of that new-found relationship, I said to him, 'Lord, I want this heart of mine to be yours. I want you to settle down here and be fully at home. I want you to use it as your own.'"

Conversations in the Living Room

In his booklet, Robert Munger describes rooms in his heart, like the library of thoughts, the dining room of desires, the living room of fellowship, the work room of abilities, and the recreational room of activities. He has invited into his heart the Christ who wants to develop a growing, closer relationship with him. Christ does this through the fellowship of his Spirit.

Speaking in the first person, Bob Munger invites him into the living room of his heart. Christ says, "Indeed, this is a delightful room. Let's come here often, and we can have good talks and fellowship together. Let's open a book of the Bible and read it together. He would unfold to me the wonder of God's saving truth and make my heart sing as he shared all he had done for me and would be to me. Those times were wonderful. Through the Bible and his Holy Spirt he would talk to me. In prayer I would respond."

But over time Bob neglected these conversations together. Christ observed that "you have been thinking of the quiet time, of Bible study and prayer, as a means for your own spiritual growth. This is true, but you have forgotten that this time means something to me also. Remember, I love you. Just to have you look up into my face warms my heart. Don't neglect this hour if only for my sake."

And so the conversations can go, as we invite the Spirit into other parts of our heart with its desires, abilities and activities. He wants to draw our whole inner being closer to God. We invite him to take over more and more of our life. That is the sanctification process.

Pietist Influences

Pastor Munger writes out of what is called the pietist heritage of Protestantism. Its roots are in the 18th century. Pietism has always been controversial in the context of church life. Because it is so subjective, it can easily be criticized, especially by those whose focus is on objective doctrine. Indeed, it is easy to mock because of its emphasis on personal experiences.

The last century has been a time of mocking. Generations of seminarians have been taught that Pietism is bad. Why? Because it too easily degenerates into an unhealthy emphasis on the behaviors that result from the regenerated heart. Key to that older emphasis is to live in ways that resist temptations, like not dancing or attending theater and movies—as if these lifestyle choices became the basis of our relationship with Christ.

The essence of Pietism was explained by Johann Arndt in the 17th century. "True knowledge of Christ is ignited by the Holy Spirit in our hearts as a new light that becomes ever brighter and clearer. A man is newborn in his conversion if the righteousness of Christ is given to him through faith. Then the image of God will be daily renewed. He is not yet, however, a perfect man but a child who must yet be trained by the Holy Spirit and day by day become conformed to Christ Jesus." I offer a more complete perspective on Pietism in my book *Your Encounters with the Holy Spirit.*

Pietist Impulses in a Church Body

Timothy Keller's writings about church ministry are currently very popular among young Evangelicals. He is Founding Pastor of the mega-church Redeemer Presbyterian Church in Manhattan. Here is what he says about pietist influences in the context of other emphases in Protestant churches:

"The pietist impulse puts the emphasis on the individual and the experiential. Pietists do ministry through church courts, but they are also supportive of ministry through para-church ministries. Pietists stress core doctrine over secondary ones and feel more like part of the broader evangelical movement than do doctrinalists. This branch, like the doctrinalists, are generally suspicious of the third branch that emphasizes social justice and culture engagement. While the doctrinalists fear culture accommodation, the pietists are more afraid that it will detract from the pietists' main concern—evangelism, mission and church growth."

I have suggested the term Guardians for the doctrinalist position and Missionaries for the Pietist orientation. The tension between the two is healthy.

The Spirit **Sanctifies** God's People

REFLECTION 40

Live the Joy of Participating in the Sacred Romance

We can try to measure sanctification and to chart individual journeys. Consider now the softer approach of appreciating the romance of being drawn closer to the heart of God. The book *Sacred Romance* by Brent Curtis and John Eldredge is a favorite of mine.

Curtis and Eldredge invite us to think about our relationship with God as a fairy tale—a true one. God is the hero who comes to the rescue of the brokenhearted. The truth of the Gospel is intended to free us to love God and others with our whole heart. Our heart is the key to the Christian life.

Scripture has three words for love. We learn about brotherly love of *philos* and the unconditional *agape* love that is our goal in relation to others. The third kind we mostly skip over—the romantic love of *eros*—because that goes to sexual attraction. But Curtis and Eldredge invite us to pause and reflect on the longing to be attracted to another.

We Are Being Wooed

That longing is the setting for the Sacred Romance. Like any good fairy tale, the hero comes to the rescue of his beloved. God the Father is the author of this romance and God the Son is the lead character. We need to be delivered from the Arrows of life that inflict harm on us and cause us to pull away from the prince who wants to rescue us.

We wonder what God is up to in the events in our lives. Curtis and Eldredge propose, "The process of our sanctification, our journey rests entirely on our ability to see life from the basis of that question. Our lives are not a random series of events; they tell a Story that has meaning. We aren't in a movie we've arrived at twenty minutes late;

156 | David S. Luecke

we are in a Sacred Romance. There is something wonderful that draws our heart; we are being wooed. Who are we, really? We are not pond scum, nor are we the lead in the story. We are the Beloved; our hearts are the most important thing about us."

Curtis and Eldridge claim we have lived for so long with a propositional approach to Christianity we have nearly lost its true meaning. Rather we should see Scripture as a cosmic drama—creation, fall, redemption, future hope—dramatic narratives you can apply to all areas of life. "Our rationalistic approach to life has stripped us of a faith that is barely more than mere fact-telling. Modern evangelicalism reads like an IRS 1040 form: It's true, all the data is there, but it doesn't take your breath away. They do not force us to our knees in reverence and awe, as with Moses at the burning bush or the disciples in the presence of the risen Christ."

The Big Picture of the Sacred Romance

According to Curtis and Eldredge, the big-picture Sacred Romance, began "Once up a time," long ago with God in loving relationships between Father, Son and Holy Spirit. Before our smaller stories began there was something wonderful already going on.

That's Act I His Eternal Heart. Act II is his Heart Betrayed. The angel Lucifer, as Satan, turned on his Maker and gained traction with others in the heavenly realm with the idea that God doesn't have a good heart.

Act III is His Heart on Trial. God puts his heart on trial in the flurry of dramatic actions we call "creation." What were his motives? Paul explained God's intentions in the first chapter of Ephesians. "In him we were also chosen, having been predestined according to the plan of him who works out everything in conformity with the purpose of his will, in order that we, who were the first to hope in Christ, might be for the praise of his glory" (Ephesians 1: 11-12).

In order for a true romance to occur, we have to be free to reject him. After the Fall, we live now our own small tarnished lives that leave us unfulfilled; we settle for just getting through the daily and seasonal routines of our lives.

Act IV is Heaven, the continuation of the Story that has interrupted by Fall. God made the earth and entrusted it to us, to bring order and increase beauty. "That arrangement was corrupted by the Fall so that the earth no longer responds to our leadership as it once did. When Christ accomplished our redemption, he didn't do it to place us on the bench for eternity. He restored us to put us back in the game."

He calls us to participate in helping the kingdom of God break into the lives around us. Paul's prayer is that the God of glory "may give you the Spirit of wisdom and revelation, so that you may know him better. I pray also that the eyes of your heart may be enlightened in order that you may know the hope to which he has called you, the riches of his glorious inheritance in the saints, and his incomparably great power for us who believe" (Ephesians 1: 17-19).

What Does God Want from Us?

We've been offered many explanations. "From one religious camp we're told that what God wants is obedience, or sacrifice, or adherence to the right doctrines or morality. Those are the answers offered by conservative churches. The more therapeutic churches suggest that no, God is after our contentment, or happiness, or self-actualization or something else along those lines. He is concerned about all these things, of course, but they are not his primary concern. What he is after is us—our laughter, our tears, our dreams, our fears, our heart of hearts.

The Still Small Voice

When the prophet Elijah was worn out and in need of restoration, he did not hear God in a great wind or earthquake or fire. Finally, he heard a "gentle whisper" in which he found God. God today desires to talk with us in the quietness of our own heart through his Spirit, who is in us. It is his voice that has whispered to us about a Sacred Romance, something much bigger than my distractions that keep me focused on details of my life. The Spirit is wooing us to realize there is something more to my life than the routines I have settled for. He is wooing us to a closer relationship with Christ.

Without the Spirit's whispers urging us to look for something more in our life with God, making progress in the life of sanctification is not going to be appealing. Our hearts have to be in the effort. It is not within us to change our sin-oriented hearts. We may want to rely on will power, but that won't last long and is likely to turn the journey into something grim.

The journey of sanctification is more likely to engage our hearts when we realize the much bigger story of what God wanted our relationship with him to be like in Act I of the Sacred Romance. Appreciating his wooing love can arouse our hearts of love to participate in the joy of sharing his love with others. We are part of something much bigger.

Conclusions

Turning Insights into Actions to Regain Spiritual Energy

The best research on congregational life reaches this simple conclusion: **Highly effective congregations have leaders with the key attribute of an unrelenting, uncompromising focus and drive to help grow people into disciples of Christ.** The strategies and programs they pursue are not radically different from those found in most churches. It's their hearts—consumed by Christ—that make the difference.

I have spent the last four years writing and distributing 120 blog articles, and over the years I've published now 18 books, all on church leadership and half of those featuring the Holy Spirit. The present 40 Reflections have the basic purpose of challenging conventional thinking about what is important in leading church life today. As always, my focus is on the traditional mainline church bodies that were so dominant in America before starting their fifty-year decline that seems to only be accelerating. Meanwhile, so many independent community churches are growing in numbers and participation. My training and inclination are to analyze why. Why are mainline churches declining and more progressive churches growing? I firmly believe insights can shape action.

My conclusion is that the old traditional churches have a Spiritual problem, spelled with a capital S for Spirit. They (we) have not paid enough attention to the Holy Spirit, who is Christ's Spirit with us now. I advocate renewed study of the centrality the Spirit had in the Apostle Paul's understanding of the church life emerging under his leadership.

What follows are eight actions that pastors and church leaders can take to regain vitality in their congregations. None of these are radical.

1. **Emphasize the basics of how the Holy Spirit influences the lives of Christ's followers.**

   Teach participants to recognize the Spirit at work in their lives. This will mean highlighting personal experiences, something avoided in traditional churches. Many pastors themselves will need to seek help learning this skill. Some experts claim that the Christian church worldwide is now growing faster than any time in its history. Almost all this is in Pentecostal forms. If you are going to be a follower of Christ, then do it in a way that produces difference in your life now. Many Pentecostals go to excess in highlighting feelings. The traditional emphasis on reason is a valuable corrective. Learn to appreciate the centrality of the gifts of the Spirit in Paul's approach.

2. **Stress the authority of inspired Scriptures**.
   We can look at the latter part of the 20th century as a great experiment with interpreting the Bible. It amounted to applying scholarly methods of treating Scriptures like any other human literature, without a faith commitment to its supernatural origins. Basically, it has been a big failure, judged by the emptying out of churches that offered this anemic view of God's Word. Where Protestant is growth is happening, it is in conservative churches. The "market" for church life is among people who are looking for a source of authority for how to live their lives. The highest quality research on personal faith growth concludes that nothing has a greater impact on spiritual growth than reflection on Scripture.

3. **Build church fellowship around encouraging one another in their Christian walk.**
   Traditional mainline churches typically have a shallow view of church fellowship where social small talk prevails. Help participants learn to talk about what God is doing in their lives. This comes easier when participants learn to recognize the Spirit's work. Help others model conversation about their walk with the Spirit.

4. **Practice personal spiritual self-awareness that helps you grow in denying self and trusting God.**
   Pastors cannot lead others to where they have not gone themselves. Pray for the Spirit's influence to grow in your life and work. Find approaches that work best for you. You will know when you are on

the right path when you find enjoyment in your ways of exposing yourself to the Word that conveys the Spirit.

5. **Call others to a personal relationship with Christ, not just to a church culture.**
Traditional mainline churches have their own distinctive cultures. "Involvement" is not necessarily a good predictor of closeness to Christ. Those open to church life today want spiritual nourishment.

While the proportion of the American population who claim no religious affiliation has increased rapidly in recent years, these typically are still open to religion, just not in its traditional institutional forms. They are looking for God-focused relationships. The fields really are ripe for harvest by those who can communicate the Gospel basics in personable ways. The unchurched looking for formal institutionalized worship are few. Pray for a fresh movement of the Spirit.

6. **Build up basic Christ-centered fellowships by reducing barriers to the Spirit's work in a congregation.**
The Holy Spirit works through the primary relationships of those gathered as a congregation. The formal constitutional structure is secondary. Its purpose is to promote the health of the informal fellowships. Organizational structures imported from secular organizations are inadequate for building up the ministry of Spiritually gifted members. Poor organization can quench the Spirit's work among participants.

Changing any organization's culture is difficult and prone to conflict. It needs to be led from the top. Start with small changes within the pastor's authority. Build on successes. Recognize that big church structures do not necessarily work well in small churches. Do what best enables participants to minister to others.

7. **Emphasize learning from experiences of the Spirit in the past and now.** You can't help people learn to swim very well by giving lectures on good swimming. Yet that is how traditional churches approach enlightenment by the Spirit. Mainline churches have a rich heritage of doctrine, or teachings *about* God. But the greater truth is personal encounters with God, guided by biblical truths. We know how to describe experiences of biblical characters. Supplement those by sharing stories about faith journeys in our times.

8. **Approach sanctification as letting the Spirit draw believers closer to Christ.** It is what happens after the Spirit by grace imparts saving faith. The goal of congregational life is to help participants grow in love, joy, peace and the other quality-of-life fruit the Spirit can produce. Life together is a process of helping each other keep in step with the Spirit. A practical way to do that is to help participants chart their own personal spiritual journey in terms of how close to or far from God they were at various stages of their life. The question then is where they want to be in the future.

None of these recommendations are an easy fix for what ails so many mainline churches. Ultimately, they involve a re-orientation of Reformation theology to the Apostle Paul's understanding of the Holy Spirit's work among God's people. The ongoing numeric decline of churches in that heritage should lead to greater humility and willingness to relearn basics of ministry.

Faithful churches are stewards of God's mysteries. How the Spirit works is a great mystery. Look for how he is working in thriving churches. Learn to let him reshape the traditional ministries that may be losing effectiveness in today's society.